IMAGES
of America

BONITA

The most famous image of Bonita is the "Old Red Barn" photograph of the former packinghouse of the Sweetwater Fruit Company on Bonita Road, taken by fire chief Jim Jones in 1959. The barn was the center of old Bonita village for many years. (Courtesy Bonita Museum and Cultural Center.)

ON THE COVER: Ann and Judy Gassaway ride their pony Comet to school in September 1948 from their home on Orchard Hill Road. The view is looking south over the Williams ranch house toward the Sweetwater Valley, which was soon to undergo a dramatic change from rural isolation to suburban sprawl. (Courtesy Molly and Steve Gassaway.)

IMAGES
of America

BONITA

Steven Schoenherr, Mary E. Oswell,
and the Bonita Museum and Cultural Center

ARCADIA
PUBLISHING

Published by Arcadia Publishing
Charleston, South Carolina

Library of Congress Control Number: 2009921926

For all general information contact Arcadia Publishing at:
Telephone 843-853-2070
Fax 843-853-0044
E-mail sales@arcadiapublishing.com
For customer service and orders:
Toll-Free 1-888-313-2665

Visit us on the Internet at www.arcadiapublishing.com

*To my father—George E. Oswell—who, in taking me to
visit every historical marker we traveled past, illustrated
that history is all around us if we choose to see it.*

—Mary E. Oswell

CONTENTS

ACKNOWLEDGMENTS

Unless otherwise noted, all of the photographs in this book came from the pioneer families of Bonita and Sunnyside in the Sweetwater Valley. Fred Higgins, Alf Lansley, Ken Milburn, the Allens, the Esterblooms, and the Carnes donated artifacts and maps and photographs when the Bonita Museum began in 1987. Many photographs had already been collected by Richard Yokley and the fire department for a display at Bonitafest. Carol Hammond from the Bonita Business and Professional Association (BBPA) and Zula Pena organized the museum's collections at its first home in Bonita Village that was provided by Phil Berdeski. After a fire in 1992 that started in the convenience store next door, the museum operated as a traveling exhibit out of the trunks of cars of museum volunteers. The museum moved to the old firehouse on Bonita Road and reorganized as an independent, nonprofit organization. A fund-raising campaign allowed the museum to move to its permanent location next to the Bonita-Sunnyside Library for a grand reopening in February 2006. The collections have grown under the care and guidance of director Vicky DeLong and the Board of Trustees. This history has greatly benefited from the knowledge and help provided by Peggy Marston, Betty Norling, Yvonne Perry, Muriel Watson, Pat Dolan, Nancy Cornell, Mark Kukuchek, Susan Hasegawa, Mary Allely, John Davies, Chuck Moore, Dan Galligan and Pam Everett at Glen Abbey, Susan Knight at the Sweetwater Authority, and museum docents Jane Campbell and Carolyn Gibbs. Bonita residents Eddyth and Mike Campbell, Betts Awes, Max Branscomb, Evaline Simmons, Al Monahan, Mario Modiano, Monica Macie, and Walter and Maria Shaw invited us into their homes and shared their personal stories. Our special thanks to Molly and Steve Gassaway, who provided their unique perspectives for this project. Steve passed away as this history was being written, and we honor his memory with the publication of this book.

INTRODUCTION

According to one local resident, Bonita is more a state of mind than a location. Largely rural but surrounded on all sides by cities, in many ways, Bonita's unique landscape, rather than its boundaries, is what defines it. Visit Bonita, even in the 21st century, and you will encounter an unusual hybrid of open spaces and suburban living. Through boom and bust, abundance and deprivation, agricultural prosperity and natural disaster, Bonita's unique setting is a product of over 100 years of history.

During the time of the Kumeyaay, the landscape of Bonita was very different. The only structures were short huts made of willow poles and leaves that were designed for seasonal travel. The Kumeyaay lived a seasonally nomadic lifestyle in the coastal and mountain regions of Southern California. The local Native Americans called this area Apusquel; the Spanish later called it La Purisma. Archaeological finds suggest that the Kumeyaay lived on the mesas surrounding the river and quarried stones for tools near the Sweetwater Dam.

The arrival of the Franciscan Friars in 1769 and the establishment of the missions of Alta California had a profound effect on the local people. The Sweetwater Valley was made part of El Rancho del Rey, the Ranch of the King of Spain, which was set aside to raise cattle that would in turn supply the soldiers and other officials of the Spanish government who were living at the Presidio. Though the area was part of the Spanish kingdom, few Spaniards lived in the valley other than those necessary to oversee the cattle operation, and no structures have survived from this period.

When Mexico achieved independence from Spain in 1821, land that had been in the hands of the missions was soon being awarded as land grants. In 1845, the parcel renamed Rancho de la Nacion was awarded to Don Juan ("John") Forster by his brother-in-law, Gov. Pio Pico. Within five years, Alta California had become part of the United States of America. Between the costs of his land claims to the U.S. government and paying taxes required by the government, Forster was heavily in debt. To pay back part of the loans, Forster sold Rancho de La Nacion.

Frank Kimball and his brothers came to San Francisco in 1861. Though his business was a success, the damp air was not helping Frank's health, and in 1868, the Kimball brothers purchased all 26,632 acres of Rancho de la Nacion for $30,000. Within days, Frank started laying out a town, and by December 1869, a post office had opened in National City. Frank operated various businesses, including a brickyard, an olive orchard and olive oil press, and fruit orchards; he even raised sheep for 10 years. As part of the sheep operation, Frank created a small reservoir that was fed by the Sweetwater River during the rainy months. In his diaries, he later refers to the pond as "Laguna Bonita," a name that remained when he sold the property to Henry Cooper.

As part of his plan for the future, Frank knew a railroad connection was required, and he worked for over 10 years to bring rail service to the area. In 1879, as part of the agreement with the Atchison, Topeka, and Santa Fe Railroad that brought the rail terminal to National City,

Frank Kimball gave the railroad over 16,000 acres of Rancho de la Nacion. The Santa Fe Railroad created the San Diego Land and Town Company to oversee the development and sale of the land. Subsequently, the Land and Town Company created the National City and Otay Railroad to ferry workers and materials to the site of the Sweetwater Dam, both the transportation and the water supply being essential to selling the land in the valley.

The earliest residents of the Sweetwater Valley all came from the east looking for better health and a change of fortune. Most were businessmen who took their accumulated assets and bought many acres that were soon producing a variety of fruit and flowers. Though they were not quite gentleman farmers, they certainly made a good living on the fruit their farms produced. Both Hiram Higgins and Willard Whitney had made their fortunes in music publishing, J. C. Frisbie had owned a hardware business, and Henry Cooper had been a lawyer.

By the mid-1880s, a land boom was in full swing in San Diego County. Several maps were recorded in a plan to sell lots in Bonita and on the shores of the reservoir, but the boom was short-lived and the developments were soon abandoned. Though the land bust of the 1890s was bad for the land business, it turned out to be a blessing for the lemon business. While individual growers had success growing citrus in the Sweetwater Valley, it was not until 1888 that large-scale citriculture began. Russell C. Allen, who had come to San Diego in 1882 and settled on a ranch in Dehesa, was hired in 1888 to be the general manager of the Sweetwater Fruit Company.

The other major citrus grower in the Sweetwater Valley was the San Diego Fruit Company, a part of the San Diego Land and Town Company that had received land in exchange for bringing the railroad line to National City. By the time the land boom ended in 1890, the Land and Town Company had thousands of acres that could not be sold, so it put many of them into citrus production. In 1891, it is cited as having 483 acres in the valley in oranges and lemons. Its fruit was packaged at a packinghouse in National City.

Though most families had some livestock on their farms, the first large-scale dairy was created on the east end of the valley in 1903 when Sam Williams started his operation. Dairies grew in popularity after 1910, and they remained a part of the valley until the 1970s. Chickens also thrived in the valley climate, and several poultry farms existed into the 1950s. The riverbed, which was dry for many months at a time, was planted in vegetables and other seasonal plants—prior to 1900 by Chinese immigrants and later by Japanese and Mexican truck farmers.

The dawn of the 20th century ushered in a decade of relative weather calm in the Sweetwater Valley. Rainfall averages were normal or slightly higher, and the citrus industry flourished, sending hundreds of carloads of lemons and oranges east each year. In 1913, however, an unusual weather disaster hit the valley. On January 13, a cold air mass that lasted for two days hit the region, leaving overnight temperatures well below freezing in Bonita. Young lemon trees were completely destroyed, and older trees suffered catastrophic losses. As a result of the 1913 freeze, Eureka lemon trees, which produced their best crop in the summer, were planted to replace the destroyed trees. The previously grown varieties, Lisbon and Villafranche, had their largest crops in the late winter and early spring, which meant they had to be stored before the peak demand of the summer months.

Just as the lemon orchards were beginning to recover from the freeze, the flood of 1916 devastated the landscape. Though the orchards were largely spared, the dam and water system were crippled, roads and bridges were washed out, the rail system was dealt a fatal blow, and the packinghouse suffered major structural damage. The time and effort to repair these systems, as well as to return the orchards to production after the freeze, kept the Bonita farmers busy into the 1920s.

The prosperity of the 1920s led to a boom in housing. Though not quite as heady as the land boom of the 1880s, the trend toward buying and subdividing land continued to grow. By the 1920s, cars had become a regular part of daily society, which opened up previously undeveloped lands where prices were lower and lots could be larger. Albert G. Wheeler, with visions of creating not "a mere residential district . . . but a residential colony" development in Bonita, purchased 319 acres and began to market Bonita Hills. Sweetwater Manor, brainchild of Edward Anderson, was a different concept entirely. Anderson bought parcels of land on the north side of the river and set about creating a small community originally using houses that were transported from a failed subdivision across the Sweetwater Reservoir.

The lack of new building from the Depression and war years created a pent-up demand for housing that raised the value of open land tremendously. In the five years following the end of the war, 181 separate lots were created for building in the valley, a veritable boom for building as compared to the preceding 15 years. Profits from growing lemons were soon to be exceeded by dividing and selling land. In 1948, Richard and Alfreda Allen created a subdivision and sold off the first pieces of the Bonita Ranch, the original holding of the Sweetwater Fruit Company. By the end of the year, they had sold off two-thirds of the west orchard of the company.

Even though these initial subdivisions consisted of large lots, with custom homes at low density, there was concern for the rural nature of the Sweetwater Valley. In 1949, a group of influential citizens formed the Sweetwater Valley Civic Association (SVCA) to preserve the atmosphere of the valley. The SVCA's first success was persuading the County Board of Supervisors to set residential zoning standard for the valley, which meant no one could build a house on a lot less than one-half acre in size. The SVCA was also successful in realigning the proposed 54 freeway away from Bonita Road in 1949, thus saving the valley floor from destruction. Yet growth continued, and many residents welcomed the new grammar school on Allen School Road, a volunteer fire department, and a shopping area with a small restaurant and a beauty parlor.

By the mid-1960s, Bonita had lost much of its character as an agricultural region and had become a bedroom community of the greater South Bay area. It had, however, avoided a single development of greater than 70 houses during this period. But the exponential growth of the region outside of the valley was soon to catch up to Bonita. Controversy followed the progress of its development, and when the Bonita Glen subdivision was complete in 1970, it contained 230 homes on lots smaller than the half-acre standard.

Out of the fight over the Bonita Glen project grew one of the most contentious battles ever seen in the valley. In September 1970, the mayor of Chula Vista sent a letter to the valley residents stating the desire of Chula Vista to annex the entire rural portion of the valley. Some residents came out in favor of being annexed as a way to retain better control of the valley, but others feared the Chula Vista government would not keep their promises and formed a group to push for incorporation. For nearly all of 1971, this issue divided the valley. Proponents of incorporation tried to stop the special election on annexation but failed, and the residents voted nearly 2 to 1 against annexation. Although Chula Vista had previously turned down requested annexations that didn't conform to the character of the valley, the mayor made it clear that from here on out, "Chula Vista would only look out for its own interests." Though piecemeal annexations had been suspended during this time, within three months of the special election, National City and Chula Vista resumed their earlier strategy of gradual annexation.

The 1970s and 1980s were to be times of great change in the valley. Paid employees replaced the last volunteer firefighters in 1968. The 805 Freeway opened in July 1975, bringing more traffic and more people. A new school was built in the valley, and a nationally known supermarket anchored a new shopping center. The valley celebrated the nation's bicentennial with a new library and post office. After a contentious battle that went all the way to the California Supreme Court, the Bonita Golf Course was annexed to National City and a regional shopping mall and movie theater opened in 1980.

Although the valley was changing, local pride was expressed in the annual Bonitafest celebration. In 1973, Emily Ritter and Beth Marks created the Bonita Business and Professional Association. Emily suggested that they do something to get noticed like have an Oktoberfest, and Adelle Rockwell suggested they call it "Bonitafest." Out of a hope for increased visibility for the Bonita Business and Professional Association, Emily Ritter and her dedicated compatriots created a celebration of what makes Bonita special.

Though Chula Vista and National City did succeed in annexing and urbanizing portions of the valley, due to the efforts of the residents, a measure of the rural character of the valley does remain. Nearly 1,000 acres of the valley are permanently preserved as open space, including much of the riverbed. Three stables still operate, and horses are not an uncommon site on the miles of trails that crisscross the valley. Some important buildings have been lost, but many of the significant houses and businesses of the past have been preserved, and though large subdivisions were built, acre and half-acre lots remain on the mesas and hills. If nothing of major consequence occurred in the valley during the last 100 years, the fact that Bonita endures in the 21st century is a significant achievement.

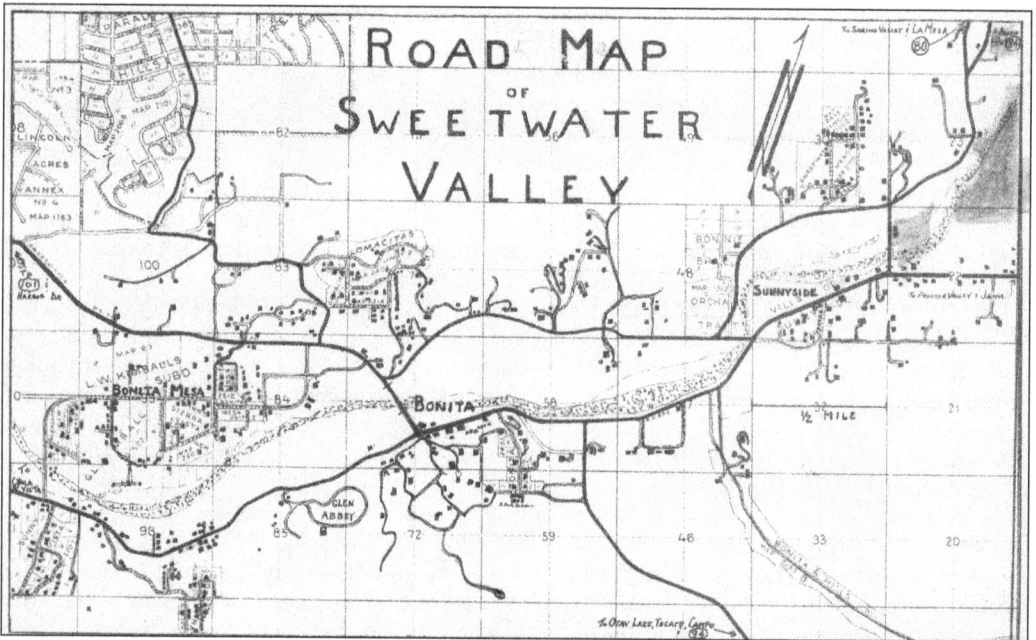

Richard Allen drew this map of the valley in 1950 when the population was about 500 in an area of 10 square miles. He was able to plot every house in the valley, along Sweetwater Road north of the river and Bonita Road south of the river. Fifty years later, the population was 17,379 living in 5,950 homes. See page 82 for the back side of this postcard map.

One

THE SWEETWATER VALLEY

The river that formed the Sweetwater Valley began in the Cuyamacas and flowed for 70 miles to the San Diego Bay. The name "Sweet Water" came from stories told by the Kumeyaay, who were the first residents of the valley. The Spanish and Mexican names for the river were different, but the American maps after 1848 made official the name from the old legends. The river was an important reason the Spanish grazed cattle there in the 1790s and why Frank Kimball bought the Rancho de la Nacion in 1868. The water drew Kimball to plant San Diego's first eucalyptus trees in the valley, as well as his famous olives and his experimental potatoes for the Department of Agriculture. Kimball not only promoted the valley's agriculture but also its climate. Many of the early settlers came for their health. Hiram M. Higgins, who planted the first citrus orchard in the Sweetwater in 1871, was a successful music publisher in Chicago but came to California to improve his health. He spent three months looking around San Diego with a soil expert for the best orchard land and picked the Sweetwater as his favorite. The Bonnie Brae of Scotsman Higgins was the first of the four ranches that established the reputation of the Sweetwater for high-quality fruit and healthy lifestyle. Willard W. Whitney built the Highlands in 1873, Judson C. Frisbie started Sunnyside in 1876, and Henry E. Cooper's Rancho Bonita gave a name to the little village that began to grow along Bonita Road. E. F. Wells came from New York in 1883 to find a healthy climate and settled in a pleasant grove of cypress and mulberry trees along Sweetwater Road where Rohr Park is today, rebuilding an old adobe house that had been built years earlier, perhaps by John Forster. His Interlaken fruits were successful, and the orchards were continued by the next owner, Dr. Frank A. Dunbar, who opened a home for invalids. The adobe home was damaged in the 1916 flood, but the valley continued to attract new residents seeking improved health or fertile land to start a ranch.

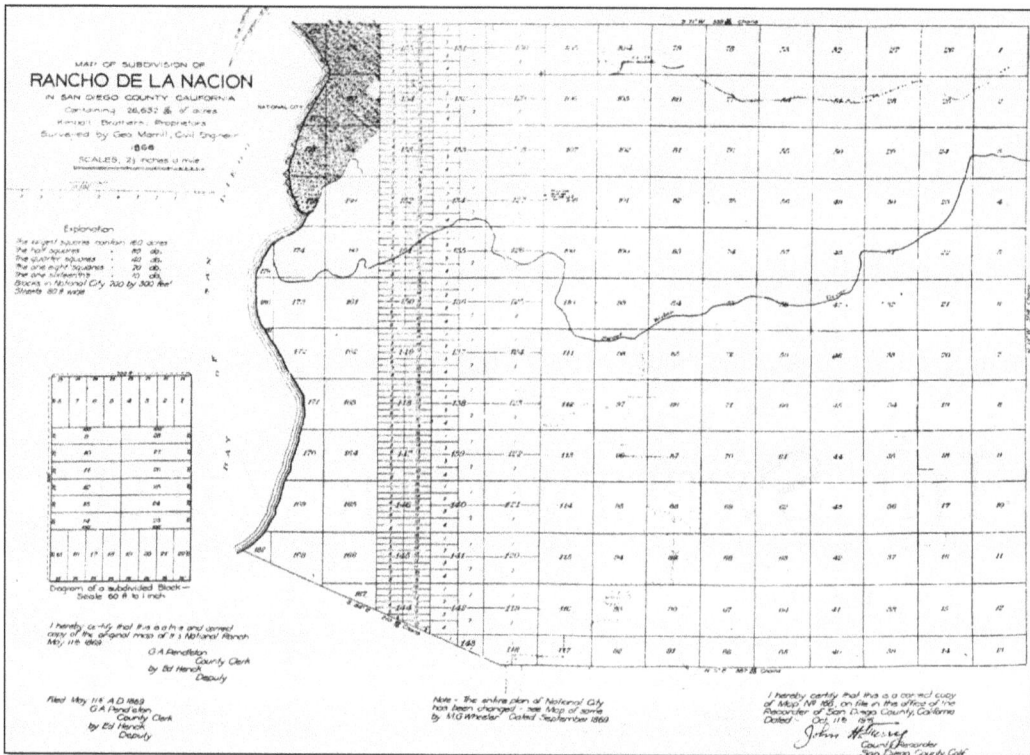

MAP OF SUBDIVISION OF
RANCHO DE LA NACION
IN SAN DIEGO COUNTY CALIFORNIA
Containing 26,632 ¾ of area
Kimball Brothers, Proprietors
Surveyed by Geo. Morrill, Civil Engineer
1868
SCALES, 2½ inches a mile

Explanation
The largest squares contain 160 acres
The half squares · 80 do.
The quarter squares · 40 do.
The one eight squares · 20 do.
The one sixteenth · 10 do.
Blocks in National City 200 by 300 feet
Streets 80 ft wide

Diagram of a subdivided Block —
Scale 50 ft to 1 inch

I hereby certify that this is a true and correct
copy of the original map of the National Ranch
May 11th 1869
G. A. Pendleton
County Clerk
by Ed Henck
Deputy

Filed May 11th A.D. 1869
G. A. Pendleton
County Clerk
by Ed Henck
Deputy

Note - The ending plan of National City
has been changed - see Map of same
by M.G. Wheeler Dated September 1869

I hereby certify that this is a correct copy
of Map N° 166, on file in the office of the
Recorder of San Diego County, California
Dated · Oct. 11th 1915
John H. Alessey
County Recorder
San Diego County, Calif.

In 1868, Frank Kimball commissioned George Morrill to make the official survey of the National Ranch that laid out quarter-section squares of 160 acres each, numbered from 1 in the northeast corner to 182 in the southwest corner. Bonita would be in quarter section (QS) 84, Sunnyside in 31, and the Sweetwater Dam in 3.

John Forster was an Englishman who came to California in 1833, married Ysadora Pico in 1837, and received the Rancho del Rey land grant from her brother Gov. Pio Pico in 1845. Known in California as Don Juan Forster, he lived at his San Juan Capistrano and Santa Margarita ranches. He built an adobe in the Sweetwater Valley but did not live there.

The Bellinger-Milburn house at 6034 San Miguel Road was built in three parts. The front of the home, with its octagonal corner parlor topped with a bell-shaped roof, was built by William and Etta Bellinger in 1896. They were adding to a second part of the house built in the 1880s by Frank Kimball. (Courtesy Ken Milburn.)

The first part was a cabin 14 by 18 feet, built by Frank Kimball in 1868 for his surveyors. It is shown here still standing as the back room of the house that Ken and Ruth Milburn restored in 1984. This room was Kimball's cabin and is the oldest structure in the Sweetwater Valley. (Courtesy Ken Milburn.)

13

In 1873, Willard W. Whitney bought 92 acres from Kimball for $35 per acre and built his Highlands ranch on a mesa north of the Sweetwater River in QS 23. In 1874, he built the two-story house shown above in a photograph from the 1880s. The house was torn down in 1961 for a subdivision.

This 1924 aerial shows the east end of the valley, with numbers identifying the (1) W. W. Whitney house, (2) Ellis Baron ranch, and (3) Sweetwater Reservoir behind the dam. Next to the Whitney house on Pray Street is the great Moreton Bay fig tree that survives today.

Henry M. Higgins bought 76 acres from Kimball for $30 per acre on July 17, 1871, and became famous for his Bonnie Brae lemons, named for his ranch that meant "beautiful hills." He is pictured above standing in front of the house in 1889 with his family, eight years before his death in 1897 at age 77.

This 1961 aerial shows the two-story Bonnie Brae ranch house built in 1872, still standing on a mesa northwest of the river in QS 48. The house was a social center of the community, with a series of avenues and walks radiating out from a 200-foot circle in front. It would be demolished for the Bonita Woods subdivision in 1961.

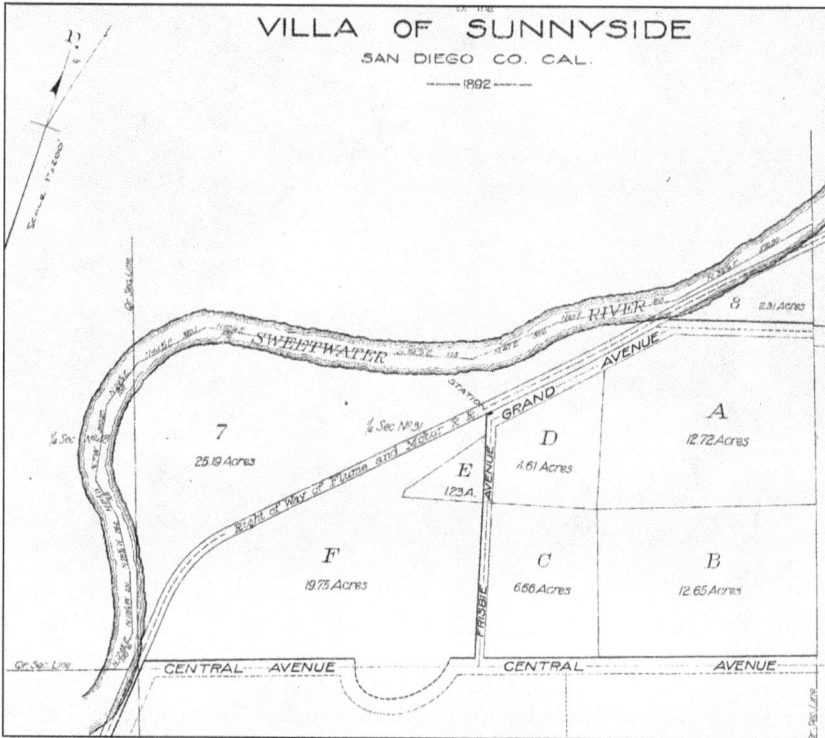

VILLA OF SUNNYSIDE
SAN DIEGO CO. CAL.
— 1892 —

Judson C. Frisbie bought 246 acres in 1876 and called it Sunnyside. He raised lemons and grapes until 1881, when he moved to San Diego. In 1890, the ranch was sold to S. W. Morgan, who attempted to create a "Villa of Sunnyside" subdivision, but few homes were built. Yet a small town developed around Frisbie Street at Central.

Sunnyside orchard and farm of J. C. Frisbie in Sweetwater Valley are shown in this illustration from Wallace Elliott's 1883 edition of *History of San Bernardino and San Diego Counties.*

Henry E. Cooper bought 119 acres from Kimball on January 1, 1884, in QS 84 and 73, and named his ranch after Kimball's pond called Laguna Bonita in the Sweetwater River. He built this Victorian-style home in 1884 up the hill from Bonita Road. It was destroyed in a fire in 1907.

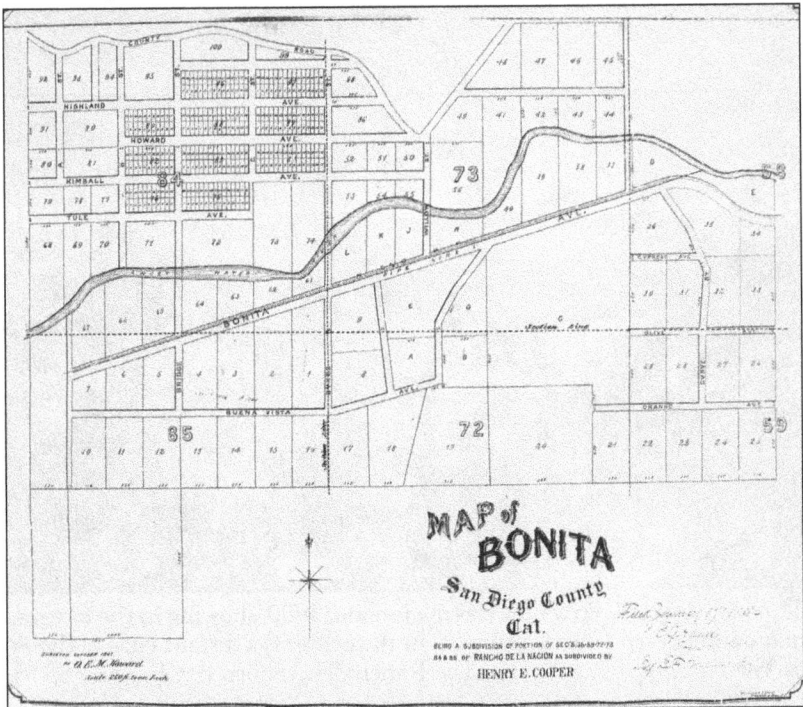

Cooper subdivided his ranch January 17, 1888, to sell lots during San Diego's great boom era, but few were sold where he hoped in the northwest corner of QS 84. Instead, he sold his entire ranch to the Sweetwater Fruit Company in March 1888, and the small village of Bonita would develop around his former home.

Alfred Keen bought a ranch in 1881 north of Cooper's ranch in what would be called the Keen Valley, and in 1887, he built the two-story house shown above in a photograph made in 1896.

This view of the Keen Valley was made about 1900, showing in the foreground the Higgins ranch house where Fred Higgins grew up; in the center is a distant view of the Alfred Keen house, and on the far right is the A. H. Ereke Ranch. The South Bay Freeway SR54 crossed this valley in the 1960s.

The citrus ranchers of the Sweetwater Valley were proud of their produce, and the export of lemons and oranges expanded after the railroad came in the 1880s. This photograph of a prize-winning orange of valley grower J. J. Mahler in the *San Diego Union* of January 1, 1915, was used by the chamber of commerce to promote San Diego produce.

This aerial taken in 1961 looks southeast at Otay Lakes Road from Allen School Road. This was one route of the stagecoach service started by John Capron in 1870 that carried the U.S. Mail from Yuma through Bonita to San Diego. Stages would use this route until 1910 and would stop at the Bonita Store before turning north at the Sweetwater Junction into National City.

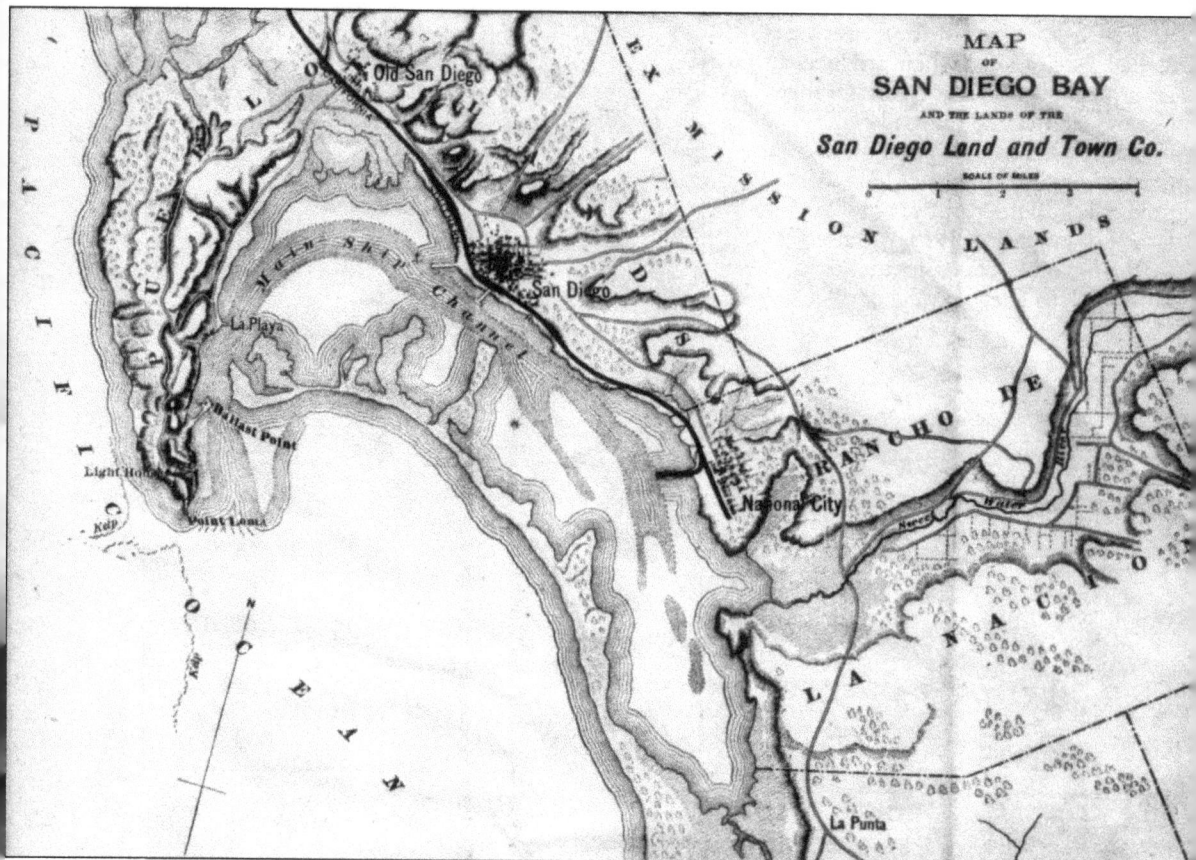

In 1884, the San Diego Land and Town Company published a pamphlet promoting "The Best Fruit Lands on the Continent," with a map of the National Ranch that featured the wide bottom lands of the Sweetwater Valley and the close proximity to San Diego Bay. (Courtesy Chula Vista Public Library.)

Two

LAND AND TOWN COMPANY

The coming of the railroad to the peaceful valley of the Sweetwater brought significant changes. Frank Kimball went east in the summer of 1880 and made a deal with the Boston Syndicate that was building the transcontinental Santa Fe Railroad to the Pacific. He gave up most of his land for a railroad terminal, and the syndicate created the San Diego Land and Town Company in 1881 to develop orchards and irrigation and a railroad in the valley. The 1880s was the boom era in San Diego history, especially after the Santa Fe lowered passenger fares to only a few dollars in a rate war with the Southern Pacific. The syndicate built the Sweetwater Dam and a pipeline system that cost more than the dam itself. The National City and Otay Railroad (NC&O) opened more land in the valley for agriculture and settlement. Engineer James Schuyler helped the company build La Presa at the east end of the railroad line. The company continued to quarry stone after the dam was completed, and Frank Kimball built the Excelsior Stone Company to crush and export material used in San Diego's growing road network and harbor facilities. The boom also attracted frauds. Alfred Isham used patent medicine advertising to sell his "Waters of Life" from the mineral springs north of the dam and bilked investors such as Coronado's H. L. Story in his Mount Gathmann Observatory scheme. Isham persuaded the daughter of British astronomer Richard Proctor to dedicate the observatory site in 1890 and again in 1896 promoted his scheme with the endorsement of the astronomer's widow, Mary Proctor Smythe. Robert Pennell sold lots in his San Miguel City that were on the slopes of San Miguel Mountain. The boom went bust at the end of 1888, and the Land and Town Company would go bankrupt by 1897, but the roads and bridges and quarries would remain. The stone used by Story's partner E. S. Babcock to build the Otay Dam in 1892 came from the Sweetwater quarry and was transported over Proctor Road, which was named for the British astronomer used to promote Isham's grand observatory.

The Land and Town Company began construction of the Sweetwater Dam on November 17, 1886. The first plan was to build a masonry wall 50 feet high and 10 feet wide at the base, but after two months, Frank Kimball told the company this was not strong enough. James D. Schuyler took over the project in 1887 and made the dam 46 feet thick at the base and 90 feet high by the time it was finished in 1888.

Stone for the dam was quarried from a nearby cliff 800 yards downstream. Boulders of up to 6,000 pounds were hauled to the site by mules and wagons. All work was done by local laborers, who operated the wood cranes and poured the cement shipped in from Belgium. Chinese workers helped clear the roads and lay the pipelines. (Courtesy Sweetwater Authority.)

Sweetwater Dam is shown under construction from November 17, 1886, to January 17, 1887.

When Schuyler took over the project, he raised the height from 60 to 90 feet, making it the highest arch masonry dam in the United States. This increased the capacity of the reservoir five-fold but covered the lands of George Neal, who filed a lawsuit that kept the reservoir only 20-percent full until the case was settled in 1891.

The only building around the dam that survives today is the Old Commissary, built in 1929 for the fishing and duck hunting recreational center at the edge of the water. "Famous Old Sweetwater" was the most popular bass lake in the county, even drawing Babe Ruth in 1927. The navy closed the lake in 1941 for sonar tests, and since 1945, the commissary has been used for storage. (Courtesy Sweetwater Authority.)

24

A man and woman in a carriage stop near the Aloha station of the NC&O railroad to view the recently completed dam, seen to the east up the Sweetwater river gorge.

On January 17, 1895, a rain of 6 inches in 24 hours caused the dam to overflow for 40 hours and pipes to break, but the masonry dam held strong as 22 inches of water flowed over the top. The dam height was then raised to 96 feet and pipes replaced, but these expenses forced the Land and Town Company into receivership.

In 1897, a drought began that lasted until the winter of 1904. The Land and Town Company had doubled water rates to recover losses, but growers refused to sign contracts with the company. Alfred Haines, president of the Chula Vista Fruit Association, argued a lawsuit that reached the Supreme Court in *Lanning v. Osborne*, but the company won the case.

The reservoir was almost dry when this photograph was made in June 1900. Water was pumped in from Jamacha Valley on a wood miners' trough shown above, and 200 wells were drilled in the lake and river bottom land, but the water had high sulfur content and damaged the trees. In 1904, the dam and water system were sold to the Sweetwater Water Company.

When William G. Dickinson (left) posed on the dam in 1888 with Frank Kimball, the Land and Town Company had launched other projects that would result in an investment of over $1 million in the South Bay. These included the International Hotel, the NC&O Railroad, and the orchard town of Chula Vista.

The final shape of the Sweetwater Dam, standing 110 feet high, is shown in the 1961 photograph. Hiram Savage repaired the dam after the 1916 flood, adding the low buttressed dam wall for a stilling basin below the main dam and building a massive siphon spillway with six tubes on the north wall.

This excursion train of the National City and Otay Railroad unloads passengers at the Sweetwater Dam. Frank Kimball noted the success of the NC&O in his diary: "There were 29,590 paid passengers last Nov. Sales and collections in the Land and Town for the first half of Dec. 1888 were $62,000."

- SWEETWATER DAM, SHOWING OVERFLOW, NEAR SAN DIEGO, CALIFORNIA.

A postcard showing the overflowing dam was popular with the tourists who took the NC&O to visit the dam in 1888. James Schuyler invested in land northeast of the dam and founded the town of La Presa, or "the dam." He also named the new town to the southwest Chula Vista, or "beautiful view."

The National City and Otay Railroad (NC&O) was built by the Land and Town Company to carry freight and prospective land buyers from San Diego down to the Mexican border and out the Sweetwater Valley to the new dam. Posters advertised the local attractions and promoted tourist excursions.

The NC&O excursion trains to the dam branched off the main line at Sweetwater Junction and followed the river east, stopping at the Munger, Lynwood, Bonita, Riverdale, Whitney, Bonnie Brae, Sunnyside, Avondale, and Aloha stations before arriving at the Sweetwater Dam, where these passengers are waiting for the train.

After leaving the Sweetwater Dam, the excursion trains crossed the Spring Valley gorge on a trestle bridge that was 70 feet high by 100 feet long and finished the 8-mile ride at the La Presa station. Upon returning to the main line, passengers connected to the Coronado Beltline that went to the Hotel del Coronado.

Lynwood Grove was a popular picnic area and railroad stop along the Sweetwater River near today's Glen Abbey. The NC&O ran special "picnic trains" from San Diego and National City to the grove for a festive day in the cool shadow of the willow and eucalyptus trees in the 20-acre park with tables and swings. Mary Allen Ward remembered the "presence of mosquitoes, large and hungry."

Frank Kimball built the picnic area in the mid-1870s near a small pond filled by the river that he called Laguna Bonita, the name that Henry Cooper later took for his ranch and home about one mile east of the pond. The circular drive around the grounds was used as a racetrack for horses. Kimball's diary noted that 1,000 people were at the grove for Fourth of July celebrations in 1887.

SWEETWATER RESERVOIR, 5½ MILES LONG, CAPACITY 8 BILLION GALS.

" HOME of Mrs. RICHARD A. PROCTOR SMYTHE   "B" to "S" HOMES of GOVERNMENT ASTRONOMERS. ENGLAND, RUSSIA, FRANCE, GERMANY, AUSTRIA, ITALY, SPAIN, TURKEY, JAPAN, CHINA, AUSTRALIA,
W ZEALAND, CANADA, INDIA, AFRICA, REPUBLICS of AMERICA.   "T" to "W" MONUMENTS OF GEORGE PEABODY, G. W. CHILDS, CHAS. BRADLAW, FLORENCE NIGHTINGALE, "FATHER ABRAHAM. COTTAGES. "X"
GRANT Jr.   "Y" CHAS. O. BROWN. "Z" Hon. JOHN F. KINNEY. "1" GEO. DAVIS "2" LAND & TOWN CO.S. 1000 ACRES LEMON GROVE "3" ISHAM'S SPRINGS of LIFE. —" THE WOLRD'S MECCA "4" WORLD'S HOME of
ISHAM'S   IN SIGHT of Mt. GATHMANN LIVE 11 MILLIONAIRES.

——————⋇ P R O S P E C T U S ⋇——————

Mt. GATHMANN | Old San Miguel | California, U. S. A.

THE SPOT DEDICATED BY MRS. RICHARD A. PROCTOR, FOR THE ERECTION OF THE WORLD'S PROCTOR MEMORIAL OBSERVATORY AND TEMPLE OF L

Mount Gathmann was going to be the new name of San Miguel Mountain east of the Sweetwater Dam, if Alfred Isham had succeeded in his scheme to get money for an observatory with a telescope designed by Louis Gathmann of Chicago. This poster shows the NC&O train heading toward a proposed gondola lift, to be the first in America, going up the mountain. The scheme failed in 1896.

U. S. Grant Jr., son of the former president, built a home on Sweetwater Road designed by William Sterling Hebbard on a 5-acre tract in 1894, near the dam. A group from Hollywood, including producer Carl Laemmle and music director Max Rabinowitz, bought the house in 1926. After 1945, it was owned by Convair executive G. Louis Farrington.

Aug. 14, 1942.
Reconstructed Trestle No.1 on 20" Wood Stave Line

The Land and Town Company built over 100 miles of pipeline from the dam through the valley into National City and Chula Vista. This wood pipe near Quarry Road was still in operation in 1942.

The tracks of the NC&O were damaged by the 1916 flood, and the railroad ceased operation. This view in the 1950s looking south shows the dirt road in Spring Creek canyon that had been the railroad line from La Presa to Bonita.

This unidentified worker is picking fruit for the Sweetwater Fruit Company around 1900.

Three

SWEETWATER FRUIT COMPANY

The Sweetwater Fruit Company was organized in 1890 by Boston investors who wanted to develop fruit orchards in the valley. Robert Winsor, R. H. Weld, and the Kidder Peabody firm bought the Bonita Ranch of Henry Cooper and hired Russell C. Allen to manage the new company. Allen moved his family from Dehesa, lived in the Cooper house until it burned, then hired Irving Gill to build his new home in 1907. Gill would be the first of several architects who were hired by wealthy landowners to build innovative and luxurious homes on the valley hillsides. R. C. Allen expanded the lands owned by the company and built a packing shed along the railroad near his home. The "Old Red Barn" as it was called became a valley landmark until it was demolished in 1960. Allen's company was the first in the county to join the California Fruit Growers Exchange, later Sunkist, the world's largest citrus marketing cooperative. Allen's wife, Ella, was a civic leader, suffragette, and one of the founders of the Sweetwater Woman's Club in 1911. The Ella B. Allen School was named in her honor shortly before her death in 1949. "It was important," Ella's daughter Mary later recalled. "At the time, there were just a lot of little ranches spread out all over here, and the club was for socializing." Mary was born in Bonita in 1897 and lived 95 years. She grew up amid the valley's countless lemon and orange trees. "My earliest memories," she recalled, "were of the sound of the little pumps all night long pumping water from the wells in the river bottom for the lemon groves." After her first husband died in 1933, she was the secretary and bookkeeper for her father's company in the Old Red Barn and was the only visiting nurse for the 500 residents of the valley. Many people owed their livelihood to the fruit company. Mike Brewer, Pleasant Wood, James Norton, DeWitt Williams, Lafe Eulitt, Tom Turner, and many others either worked for the company, sold it fruit, or lived on its land.

The Sweetwater Fruit Company built its packinghouse in 1894 on the south side of Bonita Road east of Willow Street. This view of the west end of the stucco building with "Bonita Ranch" across the top shows two empty flatcars on the railroad siding between the building and the road and the two-story Bonita School built in 1888 in the background.

From 1894 to 1916, the NC&O freight trains pulled alongside the packinghouse to load crates of lemons and oranges that the company either grew in its own orchards or bought from the other private orchards in the Sweetwater Valley.

This photograph from the early 1900s shows the packinghouse expanded and a large warehouse added east of the original barn. Mike Brewer and Pleasant Woods lived in the cottages on the right behind the lemon trees. The little outhouse in the center of the picture was a reminder that there was no sewer system in the valley until the 1960s.

This 1899 photograph shows workers packing oranges for the Hibiscus label inside the Sweetwater Fruit Company packinghouse. After packing operations ended in 1927, the barn served as a blacksmith shop, a horse stable, a feed store, and hay barn. It served as a temporary Woman's Club, 4-H field headquarters, shelter for World War II braceros, and an antique shop.

1. Shack with many Saki bottles
2. Green cottage, Woods residence
3. Mike Brewer and his mother's residence
4. Charles and Harriet Thurmond's residence
5. Unknown, this house was moved in about 1930
6. Ladd family until about 1926, then Ray Channel's residence
7. Unknown
8. Unknown
9. Sumpter Family
These cottages were all painted green trimmed in white as I
remember. The cottages should be closer to the little road where
I have the 0 number.
10. Bonita Store - Charles Haffley, proprietor, the store had a
wooden open porch facing the street. A gasoline pump (by hand)
with a glass bowl on top. It was out front, next to Bonita Road.
A small lean-to shed on the northwest corner of the store contained
motor oil, coal oil (kerosene), etc., I'm not sure but I think the
Haffley's lived in the rear of the store.
11. I believe this was a storage shed.
12. Gasoline pump
13. Eucalyptus trees (large)
14. Bonita School
15. Blacksmith Shop - George Dunham, blacksmith,
    lived I believe in Chula Vista
16. Residence - Walter (Shorty) English & family
moved in about 1930 and operated the blacksmith shop.
17. George Norton residence
18. Dick Allen's residence
19. Chapman's residence
20. Brown residence (few acres, Jersey Farm)
21. Milk barn
22. R. C. Allen residence, a large spacious building.
I remember Grandma Allen, David and Spike Allen-Charles
23. Mess hall for the Sweetwater Fruit Company workers

24. Horton Residence
25. Bridge (Bonita had two narrow bridges at the
26. Bridge (one short and one long)
27. Sheriff - George Campbell residence
28. Mrs. Carpenter's residence
29. Dunn's residence
30. Jonnie & Gloria Esterbloom's residence
    (Esterbloom Hill - John & Gloria)
31. Lemon loading ramp. Contrary to most
loading docks, this ramp was dug out so that
the truck or wagon bed would be about the same
height as the packing shed floor. Arverd Esterbloom had a new solid rubber tire truck (Master)
that was hauling packed lemons to the railroad
cars in Chula Vista in early 1920. This truck
and driver was also the first school bus to
transport us to the "F" Street Grammar School
in 1921 as the Bonita School and the Sunnyside
Schools closed down.

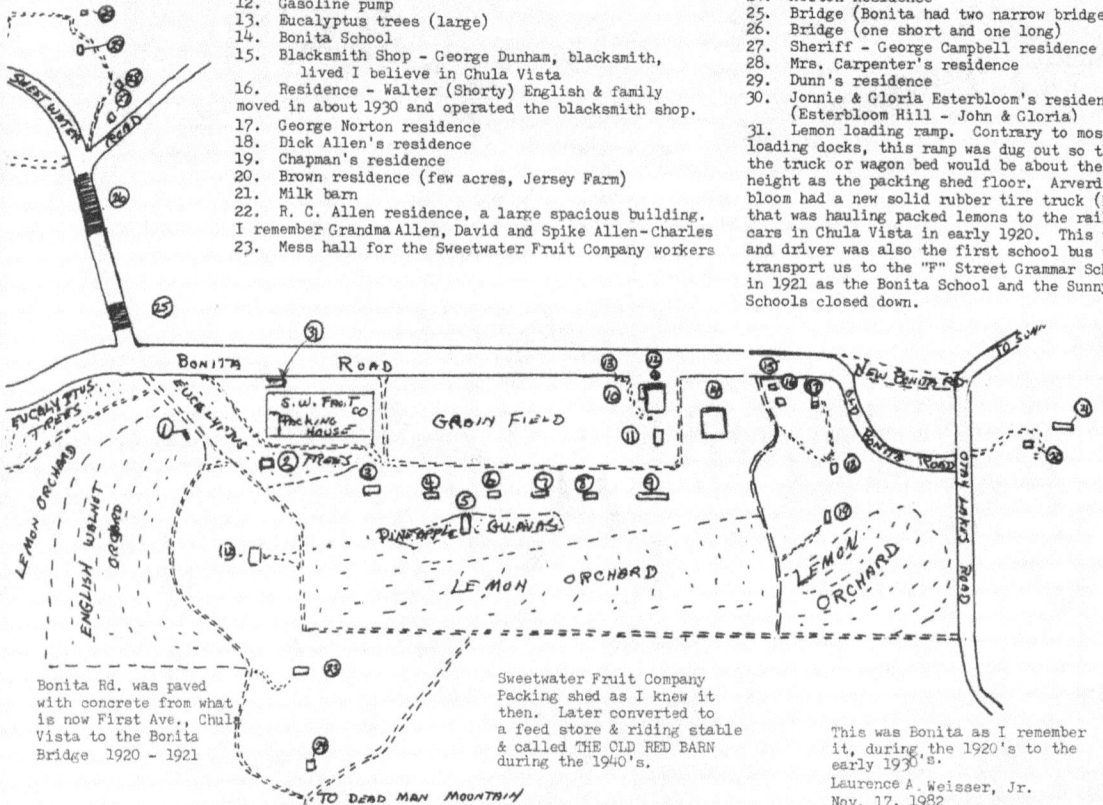

Bonita Rd. was paved
with concrete from what
is now First Ave., Chula
Vista to the Bonita
Bridge 1920 - 1921

Sweetwater Fruit Company
Packing shed as I knew it
then. Later converted to
a feed store & riding stable
& called THE OLD RED BARN
during the 1940's.

This was Bonita as I remember
it, during the 1920's to the
early 1930's.
Laurence A. Weisser, Jr.
Nov. 17, 1982

This map drawn by Laurence Weisser Jr. shows the little village that grew up around the packinghouse by the 1920s. The row of buildings behind the grain field, each painted green and white, was known as "Cottage Row," where Edward Anderson housed company workers. The old school (14) and Bonita Store (10) were on the east side of the grain field. At the top of the map at the north end of Willow Street was the Esterbloom house (30). On the right side of the map was the Brown house (20) and barn (21) of the Few Acres Dairy. Dead Man Mountain was named for a glider accident that killed pilot E. I. Shoudy on December 3, 1928.

The Sweetwater Fruit Company made elaborate crate labels to advertise and market its products. These 10-inch labels from the early 1900s were printed on paper by a high-quality limestone lithography process to produce bright and colorful images. By the early 1940s, the fancy labels were replaced by stamped cardboard boxes.

SWEETWATER FRUIT COMPANY

BONITA, CALIFORNIA.

Horse Shoe

SWEETWATER FRUIT CO. BONITA, CALIFORNIA.

During the orchard era from the 1890s to the 1940s, lemons were the number one crop produced in the South Bay. The Sweetwater Fruit Company started with the 115 acres of Cooper's Bonita Ranch and gradually became the largest citrus grower and landowner in the valley, until lemon crops declined and the company went out of business in 1957.

The Allen house was designed in 1907 by Irving Gill in partnership with Frank Mead to replace the Victorian-style home of Henry Cooper that burned in 1906. Richard C. Allen was the general manager of the Sweetwater Fruit Company and moved his family into the company packing shed until the new house was finished on April 4, 1908.

Gill's design for the Allen house called for a cement cube, fireproof, stripped of all ornamentation for classical simplicity and domestic serenity, with recessed porch and balcony. Later owners of the house have added shutters to the windows, but it remains mostly as Irving Gill envisioned, that "we should build our house simple, plain and substantial as a boulder."

Russell C. Allen is ready for a ride in his 1907–1908 Cadillac on the driveway in front of his new 1908 home. Sitting next to Allen in the front seat is daughter Eleanor Bradford Allen. In the back is his wife, Ella B. Allen, with the dark bonnet and Louise Homer with the white scarf.

In this Allen family portrait of 1923, from left to right are (first row) the boys—Charles and David—standing next to Ella B. Allen, and Richard C. Allen with arm around Alfreda's daughter Eleanor; (second row) Dorothea Allen, Morris Allen holding baby Ernest, Mary Allen, Richard M. Allen, Alfreda B. Allen, Eleanor B. Allen Mitchum, and Collis Mitchum.

The Allen house exterior was simple concrete, but the interior was well-furnished, with pecan wood floors, built-in cabinets and wainscot panels on the walls, a circular staircase to the basement, and wood beams from the Coronado ferry.

Mary Ward, the youngest daughter of R. C. Allen, was born in Bonita in 1897, married Sam Sherman in 1924, and built a house in Bonita Mesa, where she was living in 1980 when this picture was taken. After Sam died, she married Butler Ward and was honored in the 1985 Bonitafest as the oldest living native in Bonita.

The Allen house was built in a working orchard tract of the Sweetwater Fruit Company at the end of Old Orchard Lane. This view looking west from Loma Paseo shows the Allen house in back, barn on left, and the two-story boardinghouse for company workers, including 32 Japanese laborers of the Shimokawa camp that began in March 1908.

When this photograph was made about 1910, the valley was still rural. The Sweetwater Fruit Company packing shed can be seen on the right and the Allen house under two trees at the far right. The house faced east, with a view from the front door of San Miguel Mountain, on the left side of this photograph.

Boxcar No. 115 is loaded with citrus crates about 1905. The National City and Otay Railroad made daily stops at the Sweetwater Fruit Company packing plant and at the Sunnyside depot to transport fruit to the Santa Fe depot in San Diego, where it could be sent anywhere in the nation.

Lemons are made ready for shipment to the Chula Vista Citrus Association co-op plant in the late 1940s. George Simmons (left) started this orchard next to the Barrons in 1928. Mike Brewer (center) lived in one of the Green Cottages and worked for the Sweetwater Fruit Company. The man standing to Mike's right is probably his brother-in-law Pleasant Wood, who also lived in Cottage Row.

The Winsor house on Evergreen Road was built in 1913 across the valley from the Allen house. It was designed by Richard Requa, who was a partner with Frank Mead and was influenced by Irving Gill's mission-style simplicity and use of a pergola entrance with double columns. After the 1916 flood, the house was used as a Red Cross emergency shelter.

When this aerial photograph was made in 1929, most of the Sweetwater Valley was owned by the investors who had created the Sweetwater Fruit Company and the Bonita Trust. Robert Winsor was an absentee owner who bought land through the Kidder Peabody Company of Boston with his major partner, R. H. Weld.

AIR MAP OF PROPERTY OF ROBERT WINSOR, BONITA TRUST CO AND SWEETWATER FRUIT COMPANY, SAN DIEGO COUNTY, CALIFORNIA
SCALE 1:3000 BY E. RICKSON.

The Tripp house was built in 1902 as a small farmhouse on the hill above Malito Drive. Before Kate Tripp bought it in 1955, it belonged to Edward Boal, manager of the Sweetwater Fruit Company and son of John Boal, who managed the Land and Town Company and organized the Chula Vista Citrus Association.

The Smudge Shack in this 1949 photograph by Calvin Pickering was located west of the Willow Street bridge. The shack was occupied during the winter months to keep track of falling temperatures. When a freeze threatened, orchard owners were alerted to ignite the smudge pots in the fields, producing heat but also great clouds of black smoke.

46

After the 1916 flood destroyed the adobe walls of the packing shed, it was rebuilt with redwood and was called the Old Red Barn until torn down in 1960. It was a favorite subject for artists. This view was painted by Gladys Day, who was born in England and came to Chula Vista in 1929. She painted many scenes in Bonita when her daughter Peggy married Hamilton Marston.

This view of the Old Red Barn along Bonita Road in the 1950s looks to the west. The barn was torn down in 1960 and replaced with Bonita Village, the first of four shopping centers on Bonita Road, followed by Bonita Plaza at Allen School Road in 1973, Bonita Center at Otay Lakes Road in 1978, and the Bonnie Brae Center in 1979 at Central.

COMPLIMENTS OF
BONITA BUSINESS CENTER

① BONITA ASSOCIATED SERVICE

GASOLINE & OIL
MOTOR TUNEUP
GENERAL OVERHAUL
BATTERIES & TIRES
WASH & POLISH

③ LA TIENDA

FOUNTAIN LUNCH
DRUG SUNDRIES & COSMETICS
GENERAL HARDWARE

BONITA BEAUTY PARLOR

SWEETWATER FRUIT CO.
OFFICE

⑤ THE DUNGAREE

MEN'S CLOTHING
& SHOES

TO NATIONAL CITY

COUNTY HIGHWAY TO OTAY LAKES & CAMPO

PADDOCK

①

FREE PARKING

TO CHULA VISTA

② ③

HITCHING RACK

COMPANY BARN

④

MASON'S RIDING ACADEMY

④ SWEETWATER FEED STORE

HAY & GRAIN
FERTILIZER
SMALL TRACTORS
GARDEN TOOLS & SUPPLIES
POULTRY FEEDS
POISON FOR WEEDS & BUGS

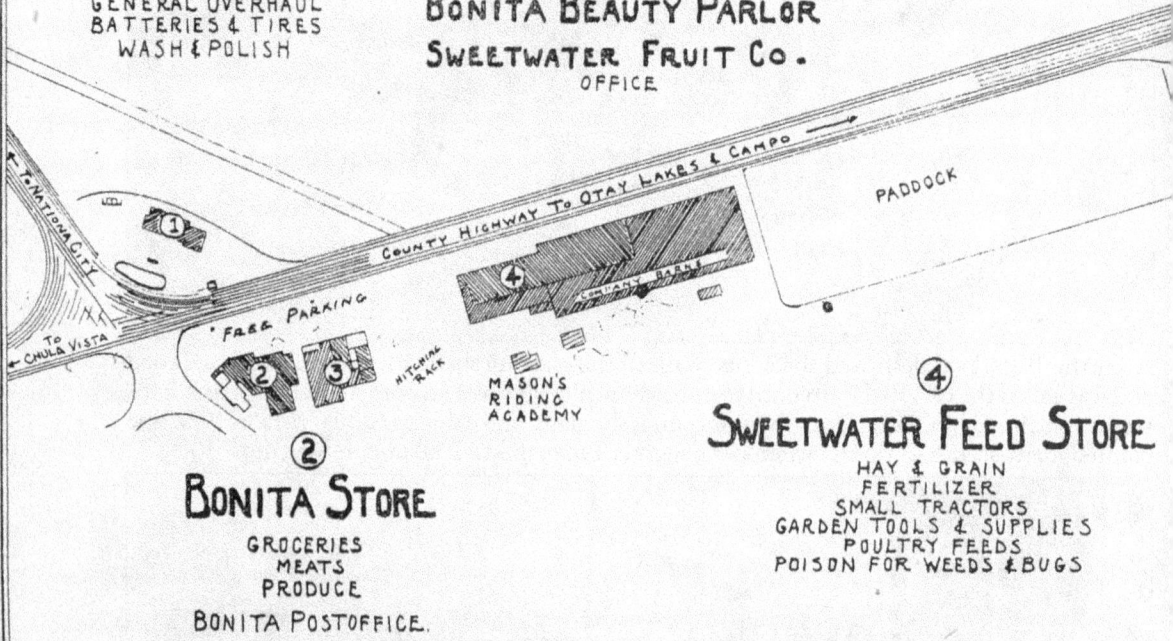

② BONITA STORE

GROCERIES
MEATS
PRODUCE

BONITA POSTOFFICE.

This *c.* 1950 map shows the handful of stores in the Bonita Business Center at Bonita Road and Willow Street when there were no shopping centers or supermarkets. Richard Allen, son of R. C. Allen, drew and printed these maps to encourage buyers to visit Bonita and purchase land that was for sale in the 1950s.

Four

BONITA'S STORES

General stores were often the first business built in any new community. In 1891, E. P. Walters opened the Bonita Store in a wooden building on the north side of the tracks of the NC&O Railroad. In addition to offering dry goods for farmers and being a stop for the railroad, in 1898, the store became the first home of the Bonita Post Office with Ilda L. Walters as the first postmistress. From 1908 to 1912, the store also housed a Wells Fargo and Company Express agent. In the aftermath of the flood of 1916, the wooden building was moved across Bonita Road and to the east, to a spot near the Bonita Schoolhouse. In the late 1920s, the business outgrew the wooden building and a new stucco building with gas pumps was built at the corner of Bonita Road and Willow Street. The stucco building was enlarged in the 1950s, and the store continued to serve the valley until it was remodeled into a restaurant. The post office moved out of the store in 1959, into the old Land and Town Offices. The Sunnyside Store also dates from the early 1890s, though the post office was established in 1892. The original building suffered major damage during the flood of 1916 and had to be rebuilt. That structure suffered a fire in 1949, started by an oil stove, which caused over $5,000 in damage to the building as well as mail and postal equipment. In 2001, the old building was torn down and replaced by a 7-11 and a CITGO gas station. The valley had a variety of fruit and vegetable stands over the years, including the long-lasting Farmer John's that started in the riverbed near San Miguel Road, then moved to Central Avenue. The 1950s La Tienda building included a beauty shop, a lunch counter, and a drugstore. In 1960, a small shopping center was built, which included a liquor shop, a dry cleaner, a realtor, and a restaurant. In 1976, the Bonnie Brae Center opened at the corner of Bonita Road and Central, with restaurants, commercial offices, a bank, and the new Bonita Post Office.

The original Bonita Store building was on the north side of the railroad tracks around 1910. E. P. Walters established the store in 1892, and his name still appears on the building. It became the Bonita Post Office in 1898, and Ilda L. Walters was the first postmistress.

In addition to operating the Bonita Store and selling tickets for the NC&O train, store manager Ralph E. Bushnell was also an agent for Wells Fargo. The store hosted a Wells Fargo agent from 1908 to 1912. The people in this photograph from 1912 are unidentified, but the woman standing could be Ilda Walters, and the car is a 1906 Maxwell Touring with right-side drive.

A train carrying hay passes by the Bonita Store about 1895. The small wooden platform was the Bonita Station of the National City and Otay Railroad, and the Sweetwater Fruit Company packinghouse is just out of the photograph on the south side of the road.

In the wake of the flood of 1916, the store was moved to a lot next to the Bonita Schoolhouse. The small structures attached at the rear of the store are the manager's living quarters, and the Bonita Schoolhouse is visible beyond the store.

The Bonita Store after the flood was owned by the Berkey brothers, Wood and Howard. The store served as a gathering place for residents, who had to travel there to get their mail as well as their provisions. In fact, home mail delivery in the valley did not begin until April 1962.

The Haffleys took over the store in 1921. When a new store was built up the road, the Haffleys rented the old building, having remodeled it into a residence.

A new Bonita Store was built in the late 1920s and was located at the corner of Bonita Road and the Willow Street Bridge. In 1936, the owners, Benjamin and Laura White, are standing in front of the store next to the Standard Oil gas pumps.

The Bonita Store was expanded under the ownership of Mickey and Thelma O'Brien during World War II. The gas pumps are still located along Bonita Road but are of the type used in the 1930s and 1940s.

This view of the Bonita Store in 1959 was just months before the post office moved out. The front of the store had been remodeled and the wall next to the doors had become a community bulletin board and advertising wall. The medallions on the sign advertised Hage's milk and ice cream from the local Hage's Dairy and Sanitary Ice Cream Company.

This photograph of the Bonita Store in Bonita Village was taken in January 1958 by Steve Gassaway before Bonita Road was widened and a stop sign was installed at the intersection. The staircase on the left side of the store leads to the manager's apartment.

Built to augment the offerings at the Bonita Store, this small brick building housed a beauty parlor and lunch counter in addition to the sundries offered at La Tienda. At the time of this photograph, the small white building on the left was home to the Bonita Post Office.

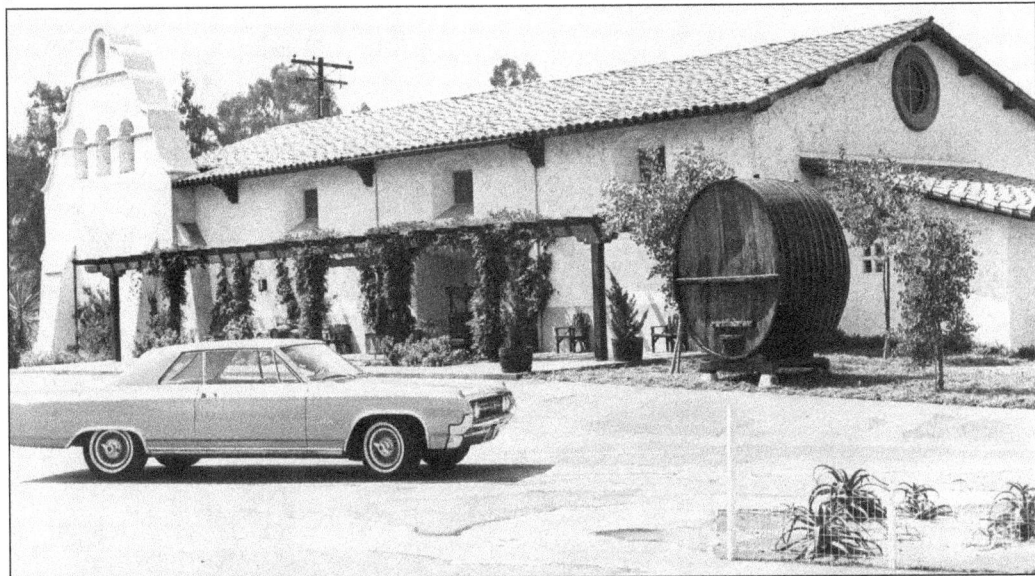

Designed by local architect Victor Wulff and inspired by the California missions, the Brookside Winery Tasting Room was finished in 1965. It was at a meeting at the Tasting Room that the idea of Bonitafest was born. The Tasting Room operated until 1970s, when it was remodeled for the North Island Credit Union.

The DiRienzos bought the Bonita Store in 1963 and ran it as a grocery store until 1983. At that time, they closed the store, renovated the building, and reopened as a restaurant that specialized in Sunday brunch and Puerto Nuevo lobster.

This aerial shows the corner of Bonita Road and Willow Street with the Union 76 gas station on the far right and the Jack in the Box on the opposite corner. The Bonita Village Shopping Center is at the top of the photograph with the Bonita Store in the middle. Much of the golf course at the bottom of the photograph is flooded.

The gas station at the northeast corner of Bonita Road and Willow Street was the Associated Service that became a Union 76 in the 1950s owned by Bill Waters. It was bought by James Emslie in 1959, when this photograph was taken, a humorous comment on progress coming to the traditionally rural Sweetwater Valley. In the 1970s, it became a Jack in the Box.

After Farmer John's Fruit Stand was forced to move from the original location under the Sweetwater River bridge in Sunnyside, it located to a lot on Central Avenue. This sketch by Joe Schmidt was made in 1984, a few years before the stand closed permanently.

The Sunnyside Store was built in 1892 at the corner of Bonita Road and Frisbie Street and acted as a station for the NC&O Railroad, which ran through the valley from Chula Vista to La Presa. The wooden building also served as a general store for Sunnyside, and in 1892, it became the post office as well, as this photograph from 1907 shows.

The Sunnyside Store was damaged by the 1916 flood and had to be rebuilt. That stucco building had a small fire in 1949 but survived and served the valley until 2001, when it was demolished. This sketch by Joe Schmidt reflects the store in the 1960s when the Wadie Deddah family owned it.

The small shopping center of Bonita Village was developed in 1960 and built on the site of the Old Red Barn. William Lumpkins, who would go on to become a well-known artist, retained many of the eucalyptus trees in the design, which included a restaurant, liquor store, dry cleaner, and a realtor.

The Southfork Steak Ranch was part of the Bonnie Brae Center, opened in 1979 in Sunnyside. Named for the Hiram Higgins Ranch located just across the river from the center, it also housed the Bonita-Sunnyside Branch Library and the Bonita Post Office.

The Sweetwater Dam withstood the torrential rain of January 1916, but the abutments on each side of the dam gave way and allowed the water to pour out of the reservoir and flood the valley. Hiram Savage was hired to repair the dam, installing six large siphon tubes on the north side and a new spillway on the south side.

Five

FLOOD OF 1916

The flood of 1916 was the worst natural disaster in the history of Bonita. It has been blamed on Charles Hatfield, the infamous rainmaker who set up a platform near the Morena Reservoir January 1, 1916, sending chemicals into the air that supposedly produced the rain that ended a four-year drought. The Weather Bureau said the rain came from several Pacific storms that converged at the same time on San Diego. Whatever the cause, the rain fell throughout the county from January 10 to January 28, causing the floods in Mission Valley and all the river canyons in the county. The town of Otay was wiped out and the Salt Works at La Punta badly damaged. The southern end of San Diego Bay filled with debris, and topsoil washed down from the hills. The rain filled the Sweetwater Reservoir until, at 2:20 p.m. on January 27, it began to flow over the top; at 4:30 p.m., the north abutments gave way, unleashing a torrent of water that rushed into the valley. The earthen dike on the low side of the reservoir also broke, sending another flood of water down the canyon past Central Avenue. A street just one block northeast of San Miguel and Conduit Roads was later named Watercrest Drive because it marked the high point of the flood waters. The railroad was destroyed, the Friends Church washed away, and the Sunnyside school damaged. The Sweetwater Woman's Club house and all its contents, including the local library, were carried into the bay. The adobe walls of the packinghouse dissolved, leaving only a skeleton building. The gardens and fields of Chinese workers were destroyed. Unlike the Otay valley, where at least 20 died that same afternoon, there were no fatalities recorded in the Sweetwater Valley. There would be minor floods in 1921, 1927, and 1944 when heavy rainfall caused the dam to overflow. But improvements to the Sweetwater Dam and the construction of the Loveland Dam by 1945 would prevent any major flooding. The heavy rains of 1979 and 1980 reminded valley residents that despite modern precautions, they still lived in a floodplain where sometimes the water was not so sweet.

The water from the overflowing Sweetwater Dam rushed through the valley, and in four hours, it wiped out the roads, bridges, and pipelines, carrying debris and topsoil into San Diego Bay, forming shoals that filled the south end of the bay and blocking ship channels for years.

The water washed away the old Willow Street bridge, but most houses in Bonita were built on higher ground and survived the flood. The house across the river in this photograph was built about 1910 and became the home of George Campbell after the flood. He bought 10 acres around Willow Street in 1917 and later donated one of these acres for the Woman's Club.

All that remained of Sweetwater Junction was twisted tracks and a half-buried streetcar of the NC&O main line that connected with the Sweetwater Line at Edgemere Avenue. Today the Second Avenue bridge crosses the river at this junction between Chula Vista and National City.

A geyser of water from a broken pipe is watched by a group of unidentified men in January 1916 near Sunnyside. The cameraman was a little shaky in taking the picture, as the water was rising and would soon cover the tracks where he stood. The valley was without drinking water for three weeks until the pipes were repaired. The tracks were never repaired, and the railroad was abandoned.

This view of the river looking south at the Avondale Station was taken March 23, 1916. It shows the damage to the station building, which has collapsed, and the footbridge that has been partially washed out. The water pipes broken by the January flood are lying on the riverbed.

The Willow Street bridge was completely washed away; only the pilings in the riverbed remain, seen on the left side of this view of February 16, 1916, looking north across the river from Bonita Road. The flood washed away topsoil, leaving behind the shallow white-topped bluffs.

Work crews repair the causeway to the new dyke a quarter mile east of the dam. This small secondary dam blocked the reservoir from flowing south into a shallow canyon that crossed San Miguel Road and Central Avenue to the Sweetwater River.

The new dyke along the southern point of the reservoir was raised to 37.5 feet high and lengthened to 1,260 feet long. During the January flood, the old dyke broke and water flooded across San Miguel Road and Central Avenue, washing away the Friend's Church and the Sweetwater Woman's Club house.

Soldiers from a local infantry unit camped near the dam to provide help in the weeks following the flood. The valley was isolated, with no transportation and no drinking water for three weeks, and the Red Cross and army provided what assistance they could offer.

Teams of horses clear the mud around the ruins of the Sweetwater Fruit Company packinghouse. The telephone poles along Bonita Road were still standing in the background, but the tracks of the NC&O railway siding along the barn were wrecked.

The tracks of the NC&O railroad lie buried in the mud covering the unpaved Bonita Road along the damaged packing shed in 1916. This photograph looking east was taken at the point where the railway siding branched to the right toward the barns, and the main route of the railroad continued straight along the road.

Trevor Adler (left) and Justin Smith found a piece of railroad track in the Sweetwater riverbed in Bonita in 1983. Another old section of track was found during the excavation for Tom Sefton's San Diego Trust and Savings Bank in 1964.

The Loveland Engineers, named for founder Chester H. Loveland of San Francisco, bought the Sweetwater Water Corporation in 1927 and built the Loveland Dam near Alpine, 18 miles upstream from the Sweetwater Reservoir. It was finished July 17, 1945, and at 203 feet high, it doubled the capacity of the Sweetwater system.

The Loveland Dam and Sweetwater Dam were owned by the California Water and Telephone Company, the new name of the Loveland Engineers after 1935. This company was sold to a Delaware group in 1966 and became known as the California Water Company. After an eminent domain lawsuit was won by the South Bay Irrigation District, the dams became a public utility in 1977, the Sweetwater Authority.

Heavy rain in 1979 and 1980 caused several periods when water flooded the lower parts of the Sweetwater Valley. Jim Thompson took this photograph of the flooded Sweetwater Park in 1980.

The golf course was underwater in the floods of 1980.

It was difficult to retain teachers in rural areas such as Bonita or Sunnyside. Margaret Clemmens was unusual because she stayed at Sunnyside for six years, from 1913 to 1919. The pay was low, only $65 per month, and the rules were strict. Female teachers could not marry or engage in "unseemly conduct," could not smoke, drink, or frequent pool rooms or public halls.

Six

SCHOOLS AND CHURCHES

Schools and churches were few and far between in rural Bonita. The little grammar schools on Bonita Road and in Sunnyside served a few dozen students until they were shut down by the new Chula Vista Union School District in 1921. Arvid Esterbloom used his Master lemon truck as the first school bus in Bonita, bouncing kids into Chula Vista and National City on the truck's solid rubber tires. After 1921, the only school in the valley was Mrs. Grace Bonnet's private boarding school until the Ella B. Allen School opened in 1947. The third Sunnyside School was built in 1959, and Valley Vista School opened in 1969. The nearest high school was in National City until the Chula Vista High School was built at Fourth and K Streets in 1950, and Bonita Vista High School began in 1966 on Otay Lakes Road. There were no colleges in the area until Southwestern Community College opened in 1964. The Sunnyside Friends Church built in 1915 was the only church in the valley until the chapel at Glen Abbey was built in 1930. Local families joined with the Episcopal Church to build the Church of the Good Shepherd in 1956. The Friends Church was reorganized in 1970 as the Wesleyan Church of the Valley and moved in 1980 across the valley, where it is now the Sweetwater Community Church. Pastor John Garrisi began the Bonita Presbyterian Church in 1971 and moved to a site next to the post office on Central Avenue in 1977. The Seventh-day Adventist Filipino-American congregation moved a worship hall to 3602 Bonita Road in 1977. Victor Wulff designed the Grace Baptist Temple at 4766 Bonita Road in 1975, but the 15-acre site was sold in 1978 to the Bonita Christian Center. Corpus Christi Catholic Parish was organized on Bonita Road in 1984 and moved to its new church on Corral Canyon Road in 1990.

Bonita School of 1888 was the first school to be built after the county Board of Supervisors approved the establishment of the Sweetwater School District. The site chosen was one acre on Bonita Road just east of where the packinghouse would be built (see page 36) and where the Big Bear Market was built in 1975. The first teacher was Mary Nichol, who was paid $60 a month to teach 23 students.

In 1890, a Sunnyside School District was formed and a small school was built at the corner of San Miguel and Conduit Roads. This photograph of the Red School House in 1892 shows teacher Georgia Knapp with her class of 24 students.

This photograph of 1910–1911 depicts the back of the Bonita school. From left to right are (first row) Hellen Moller, unidentified girl in black coat, and Donald Norton; (second row) George Dell, Blanche Campbell, John Norton holding horse, two unidentified girls, Mildred Campbell, Leonard Scott, Bessie Burtner, Omar Courtney, Fred Higgins holding a shovel, two unidentified girls, teacher Georgia Wiard, and four unidentified.

Ella Campbell was the teacher of the Bonita School from 1912 to 1917, and she is most likely the figure in this group standing in the back center on the porch in front of the school in 1916. The building survived the flood, but the school closed in 1921 when the Bonita schools were absorbed into the Chula Vista Union School District.

After the 1916 flood damaged the first Sunnyside School, a second school was built at the same location. This class portrait was taken when Margaret Clemmens (far right) was the teacher, from 1916 to 1919. When Sunnyside was absorbed into the Chula Vista District in 1921, the school was uprooted, rolled on logs down Bonita Road into Chula Vista, and put across the street from the F Street School.

Mrs. Leon Bonnet (Grace) opened a private school in 1928 in the old Winsor Ranch buildings up the hill on Evergreen Road north of Sweetwater Road. This Bonita School was a progressive coeducational day and boarding school for 12–15 students until 1933. The bunkhouse shown in this 1940 photograph had dorm rooms upstairs and classrooms downstairs.

The main classroom building of Bonnet's Bonita School was a converted barn from the old Winsor Ranch, with a full-size gym in the center and additions built on each side for classrooms. The other buildings on the 8-acre site included a theater, chapel, offices, and a converted milk house for the headmaster. A tennis court can be seen in the back right of this 1939 photograph.

In 1936, the school made a transition to a male-only college prep school, and the name was changed to the Bonita School for Boys. Under headmaster Steve Gassaway (1939–1942), the school grew to 45 students but closed when World War II began. This class of 1941 included a German refugee, the son of a British soldier, and a Syrian boy whose father was the American consul in Holland.

The Bonita School for Boys took regular trips on bicycles or in these Ford Woodys to the Borrego desert, Salton Sea, Monument Beach at the Mexican border, Mount Wilson Observatory, Griffith Park Planetarium, and the High Voltage Lab at Caltech. Horseback riding lessons were offered at the Mason Academy next to the Old Red Barn on Bonita Road.

At the Bonita School for Boys Faculty Tea in 1941 are, from left to right, James Bouey, coach James Colvin, Mary Allen, Anna Gassaway (Steve's sister), Molly and Steve Gassaway, Mr. Kiehle, John Gill, Mrs. Wimmer, and Mr. and Mrs. Jepsen.

The Sweetwater Union High School District was organized on January 20, 1920, including Bonita, Sunnyside, Chula Vista, and National City. The new Sweetwater High School was built at Highland Avenue and Twenty-ninth Street in National City, with landscaping by R. C. Allen of Bonita, and dedicated at the end of May 1922.

Bonita Vista High School was built on Otay Lakes Road after Chula Vista began annexing the area south of Bonita in 1961 to build a college. The high school graduated its first class in 1969 and achieved national recognition in the 1970s with the Music Machine performance choir, founded by Ron Bolles.

Southwestern Community College was built on 157 acres of San Miguel Mesa land that was part of the Cockatoo Grove lima bean fields of Alf Lansley and the Schutte brothers. During construction, the college held classes in Chula Vista High School from 1961 to 1964.

Sweetwater Union District superintendent Joseph Rindone Jr. (left), contractor O. L. Carpentar (center), and college president Chester DeVore (right) presided at the ground-breaking for the new college on February 14, 1963. Although many buildings were still under construction, the college opened in September 1964 and was officially dedicated December 6.

The Little Church of the Valley was a landmark for many years at Bonita Road and Dory Drive. It was built in 1914 as a Quaker Meeting House, rebuilt after the 1916 flood, remodeled in 1959 with a steeple replacing the belfry, became a Wesleyan church in 1969, and was moved in 1980 across the river to 5349 Sweetwater Road.

Pastor Rosa E. Virtue, in the center holding two books, traveled every week by horse and buggy from Otay to preach at the Sunnyside Friends Church. The Laubmayers and Chapmans started the church in a tent in October 1914 (Ben Laubmayer is far right). The DeWitt Williams family donated the carved rosewood piano in 1917. The Simmons family sold 4 acres to Wesleyan Church for a new site in 1980.

The Church of the Good Shepherd began as a Sunday school branch of St John's Episcopal Church of Chula Vista. The land came from a former lemon grove, part of which is seen on the right of this 1957 photograph. Prior to the completion of a permanent home in 1956, the congregation met in the Little Chapel of the Roses at Glen Abbey, rented for $10 per week.

Gladys Day was the wife of church groundskeeper Arthur Day and mother of Peggy Marston, who started the first Sunday school classes with her husband, Hamilton Marston, in their Bonita home in November 1953. Gladys painted this watercolor of the Church of the Good Shepherd, designed by San Diego architect William Wilmurt.

Glen Abbey began on 112 acres in 1924 by R. C. Allen, John Boal, and G. Ivan Peoples as a memorial park with landscaping by Nathaniel Slaymaker. This office building and the gates that were built in 1925 still remain at the entrance. In 1945, Glen Abbey was purchased by the Fred Davies family and today is part of the Dignity Memorial network of cemetery service providers. (Courtesy Glen Abbey.)

Built as part of Glen Abbey Memorial Park, the Little Chapel of the Roses was dedicated in 1930 and has been the site of countless weddings and funerals. The chapel was inspired by Somersby Church in England, where Alfred Tennyson was baptized, and contains stained-glass windows by the Judson Studios of Los Angeles, a prominent West Coast glazier.

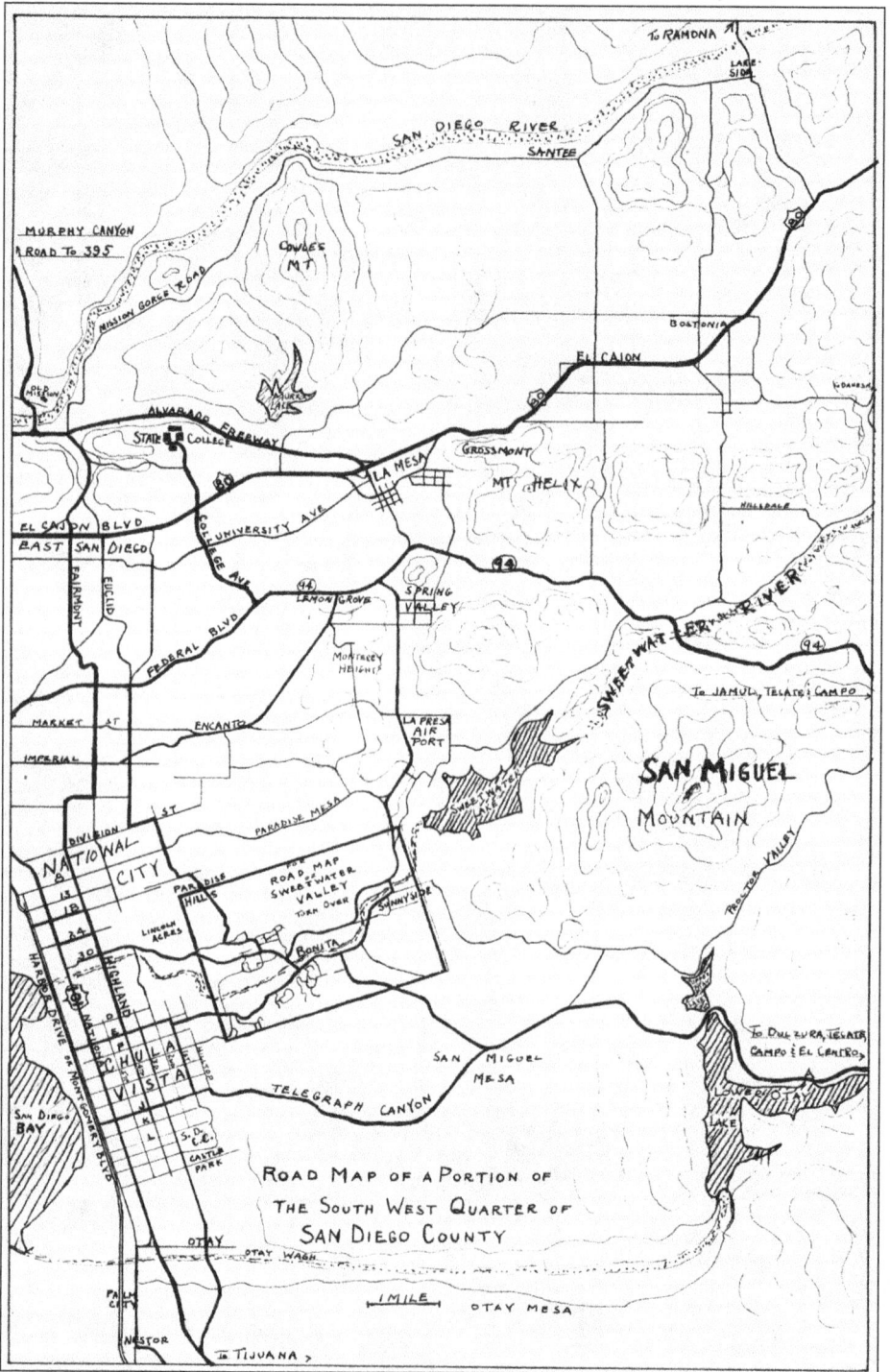

This is the back of the postcard map drawn by Richard Allen in 1950 (see page 10). There are no Interstate Highways 5, 8, and 805, and no South Bay Freeway 54 across the valley yet. Chula Vista will not begin its eastward expansion to San Miguel Mesa and Otay Lakes Road until the next decade.

82

Seven

LIFE IN THE BELOVED VALLEY

Gloria Esterbloom called Bonita her "beloved valley" when she wrote about her life on Esterbloom Hill above Willow Street on the north side of the valley. Although the population was small when she came to the valley in 1910 at age 14, she held fond memories of what she called the "simple country life" of a close-knit community. In the 1920s and 1930s, orchards and ranches would be developed by those who later would be called the old-timers. Fred Higgins and Albert Campbell started in the Keen Valley. Charles Favel, Clarence Bevel, and the Margaret Clemmens family would settle out east on the San Miguel Road. DeWitt Williams, Charles Scott, William Dolan, and Jesse Carne would build ranches along Sweetwater Road and around the old Bonnie Brae ranch. Ed Burnell, George Norton, and the Pappas family from Greece would settle on Bonita Mesa in the west valley. The homes built by these families were simple and utilitarian. Mary Allen and her husband, Sam Sherman, hired local carpenters to build their redwood Craftsman house on Bonita Mesa. Cliff May designed four buildings in the valley in the 1930s when he was developing the California ranch house style. May was a descendant of the Estudillos, who built the classic adobe ranch house in Old Town San Diego in 1835 that was restored in 1909 by Hazel Waterman for its new owner, John D. Spreckels. Waterman gave her blueprints to Cliff May, and he sought to replicate the old ranch house style. In Bonita from 1934 to 1936, he built the Dittenhaver, Whelan, and Stephens homes and the Sweetwater Woman's Club house. The Woman's Club changed during this era as the status of women changed in the nation with suffrage and new opportunities. Led by suffragette Ella B. Allen and Olive Norton, who was the first woman elected to the school board in 1921, they formed committees to pave Bonita Road and turned the old Bonita school into a community center. The beloved valley may have been rural and simple, but the people were builders of a dynamic community.

Fred Higgins (no relation to Hiram M. Higgins) was born in England and came to America at age one in 1899 with his mother, Bertha E. Higgins, to join his father, Charles Higgins, who had found a job in Bonita on the NC&O Railroad. Charles bought a lemon ranch in the Keen Valley, and Fred grew up on this ranch where, at age 4, he posed for this picture.

Fred is shown in a carriage on Revolucion Avenue in Tijuana in 1904, seated between his father, Charles (right), and a Mr. Parsonage of Sutton-Codfield, England, with their wives in back. Tijuana was a favorite day-trip destination for Americans living near the border before the revolutions of 1910–1911 made border crossing much more dangerous.

Horse riding and racing were popular in the South Bay. There were several racetracks along the border in Tijuana and Siempre Viva. Ralph Granger built the Sweetwater Race Track along the southern edge of National City, and in this photograph, Fred Higgins is racing a sulky at this track in 1912 behind his horse named Prince.

Fred Higgins played football at National City High School and in this picture wears his uniform on his Keen Valley ranch. He joined the army in World War I but did not go overseas or see any action. His mother was a founder of the Sweetwater Woman's Club, which served as a Red Cross Auxiliary during the war.

After the 1916 flood destroyed the NC&O Railroad, the only transportation in and out of the valley were the dirt roads west into Chula Vista and National City, southeast by Otay Lakes Road to Campo and El Centro, and northeast by Sweetwater Road to Spring Valley. Fred Higgins began a transport service in 1921 with this Republic truck.

Fred Higgins (right) stands with a fellow worker in 1923 ready to haul hay in his Republic truck. The sign on the side reads "Higgins Sweetwater Valley Truck Line and Intermediate Points Daily Service Phone Nati'l 137 W." The hay went to the local dairies, where Higgins would pick up milk for delivery to Chula Vista and National City early every morning.

Fred and Lucille Higgins were married in 1925 and moved from his father's Keen Valley ranch to his own lemon ranch in Sunnyside. They are shown in this photograph next to crates ready to go to the Chula Vista Mutual Lemon Association. Lucille Higgins came to Bonita in 1924 from New Mexico and met Fred at a social in the old Bonita schoolhouse, where Fred had attended as a boy from 1904 to 1912.

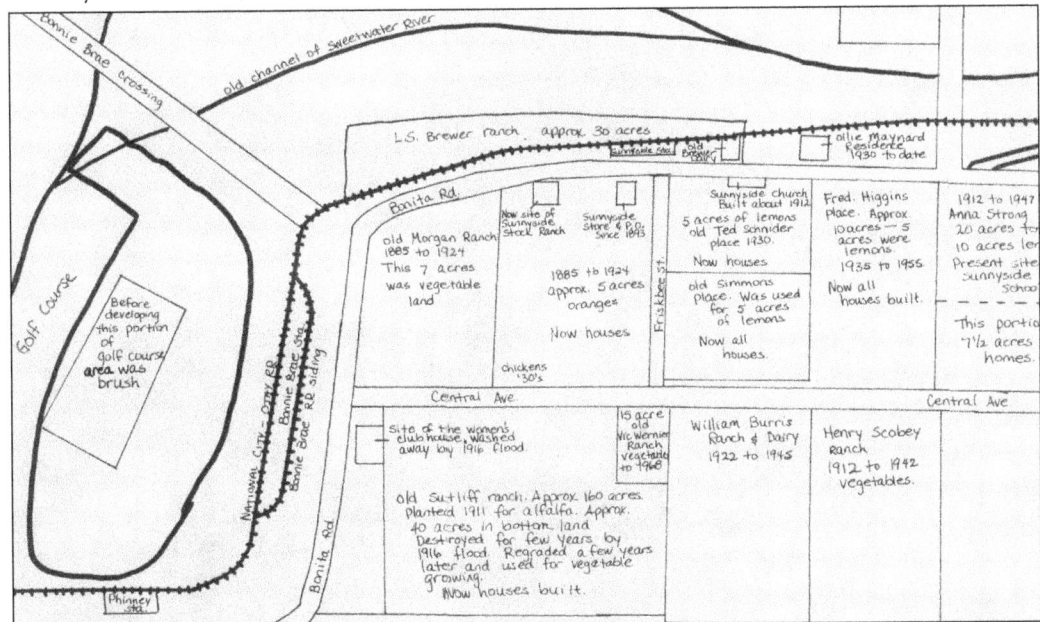

In 1973, Fred Higgins drew on a long piece of butcher paper with a red marker a detailed map of Bonita and Sunnyside, describing in his own words how he remembered it during his lifetime. The transcribed map is displayed in the Bonita Museum, and this detail shows where the Fred Higgins ranch was located on Bonita Road near the Sunnyside Church.

This picnic was held in 1903 in the orchards of the Favel ranch 2.5 miles east of Sunnyside on San Miguel Road. Charles A. Favel and his wife, Ethel, came from Ohio in 1892 and bought 28 acres for a lemon ranch. They were almost wiped out by the drought of 1897–1904, but as this photograph shows, they stayed and prospered.

Charles H. Favel was born December 16, 1891, the oldest son of Emma and Charles A. Favel. In this photograph from 1930, he stands in the ranch house garden with his wife, Ethel. The younger son was Anson C. Favel, who worked for Hiram and Vi Horton in Bonita. Daughter Ruth Favel married Mason Hagen in 1930.

Ethel and Charles Favel are smiling for a Mother's Day photograph in 1930 on their San Miguel Road ranch. Behind the steer being held by Ethel is a small calf. The hills south of the reservoir had few trees and were used for grazing the cattle of the large Sam Williams dairy near the Favel ranch.

Crates of lemons are being loaded on a truck in the Favel orchards in the 1920s. The boxes are labeled C.V.C.A. and are destined for the big packinghouse of the Chula Vista Citrus Association at Third and K Streets in Chula Vista, which was part of the Sunkist growers co-op until the packing plant was torn down in 1960.

Emma Favel sits on the front porch of her house, built at 7310 San Miguel Road in 1892. This photograph was made in 1931, and the house was eventually torn down. The Favel ranch produced lemons until 1950.

Emma's husband, Charles A. Favel, was born 1857 in Ohio and was a young man of 21 when this portrait was made. He came to California and with Emma founded his ranch on the eastern edge of Sunnyside in 1892. The twins, Ruth and Anson, were born December 11, 1895, and went to the Sunnyside School.

This view is from the porch of the Williams house, built in 1946 by Jim Williams, the son of DeWitt. It looks southeast over part of the 200 acres that DeWitt Williams assembled from 1901 until he died in 1947. He had 100 acres in lemons, a dairy, and a corral for livestock. Near the original Williams home on Winnetka were several barns, shops, and bunkhouses.

DeWitt N. Williams (no relation to Sam Williams) and his wife, Mathilde, were married in 1907. DeWitt was born in 1872 in Michigan and came to Bonita in 1891. He worked for R. C. Allen until he was able to buy the first 20 acres of his ranch north of the Sweetwater Road at Winnetka in 1901. During its 74 years of operation, it was known as the most modern and best-equipped ranch in the valley.

Charles J. Scott goes rabbit hunting in 1904 on his ranch north of the Sweetwater Road near the Dolan ranch. When he came to Bonita from England in 1889, he went to work at Finney's Nursery, became an expert horticulturist, helped with many of the valley's orchards over the years, and developed his own spray mixture of pot-ash and coal oil to combat pests.

Dorothy Scott (far right) played on the National City High School girls' basketball team in 1910. The next year, her father, Charles J. Scott, became manager of the Bonnie Brae orchard that had been started in 1871 by Henry Higgins. After the flood of 1916 and the sale of the ranch in 1921, Scott moved to his own ranch nearby and managed orchards in Chula Vista.

Rebecca Campbell emigrated to Bonita from Newfoundland in 1891 and ran the boardinghouse on the Keen ranch. Her son Albert Campbell married Mabel Hansen, and their two children were Aletha and Edwin, here picking oranges about 1917. Albert built a house near today's Rohr Manor and, during the 1920s, owned hundreds of acres of what became the park and golf course.

Frank Campbell, Albert's brother, is sitting on a 1914 Excelsior motorcycle with the new V-twin engine that made it the fastest motorcycle in the world. Frank was a machinist who became a motorcycle cop for the California Highway Patrol. Frank's other brother, George Campbell, was the local sheriff in the 1920s, and his sister Ella was the teacher at the Bonita School.

The group of girls swimming in the Sweetwater River near Sunnyside about 1917 was an example of the active lifestyle of valley women. Loren Laubmayer, third from left, was the cousin of Della Laubmayer, who most likely took this picture. Della was the daughter of Conrad and Mary Laubmayer, who owned the lemon ranch east of the Barrons on Sweetwater Road and who started the Friends Church in 1914.

The Burnell sisters—Helen (left), Eleanor (center), and Marian—came to Bonita in 1914 with their parents, Edward and Hannah Burnell, and lived on a chicken farm on Bonita Mesa Road. They walked 2 miles every day to the one-room school on Bonita Road. Helen was in the first graduating class of the Sweetwater Union High School in 1922 and went to San Diego Normal School to become a teacher.

The Ward-Sherman house in Bonita Mesa was built in 1924 by Mary Allen, the daughter of Russell C. and Ella B. Allen, when she married Samuel Sherman, the manager of the Sweetwater Fruit Company. It is a simple one-story, U-shaped Craftsman house built of redwood. After Sherman died in 1933, Mary lived in the house until she died in 1992.

The Olson house at 3522 Sweetwater Road was designed in 1927 by Edgar Ullrich as the gatehouse of a larger Spanish Revival residence. The main house was never finished because of the Great Depression, and Genevieve Olson lived in El Miradero while she ran the Caligator Company, which sold "alligator pear" avocados.

Jesse and Elizabeth Carne moved from Nevada in 1911 and bought 9 acres in what is now Bonita Woods to start this chicken ranch. Jesse took his eggs by wagon to the Bonita station of the NC&O Railroad and put them on the train for buyers in National City. His business would grow into the largest hatchery in San Diego County by the time it was sold in 1951.

Jesse Carne and his family are standing in front of their chicken ranch in the Sweetwater Valley about 1920. To Jesse's left is his younger daughter, Dorothy; wife, Elizabeth; and older daughter, Edith, who graduated from San Diego State University in 1936, became a teacher in National City until 1976, and authored two books about her life at the chicken hatchery.

Jesse expanded his business in 1923 when he opened this hatchery in National City at Sixteenth Street and Palm Avenue. Jesse put his brother Ernest in charge of the Sweetwater ranch, and the family moved to Sixteenth Street in National City. The first small incubators could hatch 500 chicks each. In this photograph, Edith Carne is sitting in the hatchery with younger sister, Dorothy (standing).

At the old ranch, the girls had been paid $1 a week to turn the eggs every day by hand, but the new hatchery would be equipped with three large incubators that produced 129,000 chicks from eggs every three weeks. Edith here opens an incubator box labeled, "To raise every loveable chick use Pratt's Buttermilk Baby Chick Food."

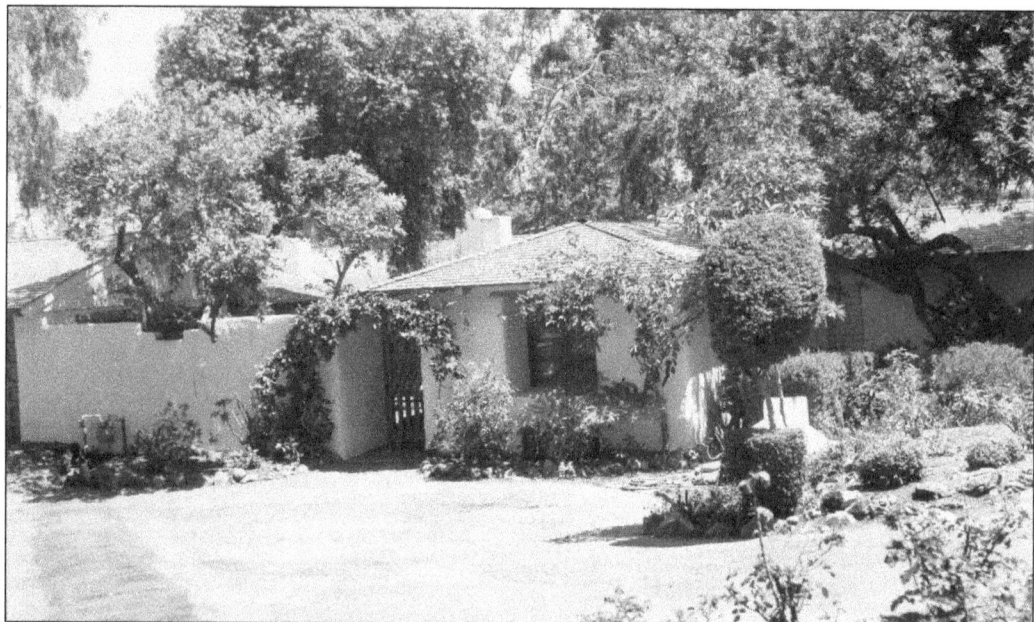

The Dittenhaver house at 3462 Malito Drive was designed by Cliff May, the pioneer architect credited with inventing the California ranch house in San Diego in the 1930s. It is a U-shaped brick and stucco one-story home built in 1934 around an inner courtyard. Dittenhaver managed Western Salt in Chula Vista. The house was bought by John B. Boal in 1943.

The Whelan house at 3597 Lomacitas Lane was another Cliff May ranch house, built in 1936 by Violetta Horton on property from Richard Allen and sold to San Diego Superior Court judge Vincent P. Whelan. The walkways are of brick, and all doorways are arched. Each room has a different pattern floor tile, a Cliff May characteristic.

Gloria Esterbloom in a white dress stands in the center of the Sweetwater Woman's Club in the 1940s at their clubhouse, designed by Cliff May in 1934. The club began in members' homes in 1911, but after the 1916 flood, the old Bonita School was used for meetings until the new rustic structure at 3855 Sweetwater Road was built on land donated by George Campbell.

The Sweetwater Men's Club was formed in 1942 as a civil defense organization and to build homes for those who needed assistance. They helped organize the volunteer fire department after the war. This Halloween party picture from the early 1950s includes founders Steve Gassaway (seated second from right) and Hamilton Marston (standing second from right).

Dairyman Walter Lamb built this house with stones from San Miguel Mountain.

Eight

DAIRIES AND HORSES

Most of the valley at one time was covered with lemon orchards or dairy pasture. There were at least 30 separate dairies between the years 1916 and 1950. The largest were the 3,000-acre Sam Williams ranch and the 500-acre ranch of William Burris on Central Avenue. The William Dolan and Levi Kincaid dairies from 1910 to 1930 took up several hundred acres northeast of the Bonnie Brae ranch on Sweetwater Road. A majority of the dairies were small operations of 10 or 20 acres and 20 to 30 cows. Walter C. Lamb came to Bonita with his parents in 1898 from Minnesota and bought 15 acres along Bonita Road near Lynwood Grove. Margaret Woodhouse remembered that in the 1920s milk from Lamb's Dairy was delivered every morning at 6:00 a.m. in glass bottles with cardboard caps, and her family would keep it cold for the day in an icebox. Walter Lamb retired in 1930, and when he was 70 years old, he decided to build a house for his daughter Alice on Holly Way overlooking the valley, made with stones he collected from San Miguel Mountain. Joining the dairies in this era were the horse farms that took advantage of the valley's open spaces. Stables such as Mason's Riding Academy in old Bonita Village bred and trained horses in the 1920s. Bob Bradley's Bonita Valley Farm at 3051 Equestrian Lane became the home of the Silvergate Riding Club, San Diego's oldest horse club, which had started in Balboa Park in 1924. Bradley's also hosted the Balboa Mounted Troop, a women's English riding group established in 1935. As more residents became horsemen, more clubs were founded. The Sunnyside Saddle Club, a family-oriented organization, was founded in the spring of 1963 by Noel Confer and his sister, Shirley. The Bonita Valley Horsemen was started by Shirley Wise and about 20 families in 1969 as Corral 89 of the national Equestrian Trails, Inc., and in 1975 became an independent local club. Equestrian trails became an integral part of the Sweetwater Community Plan that was shaped in the 1970s.

Sam Williams started his dairy in 1905 on 3,000 acres in the east end of the valley, from the reservoir (seen above at left) south to Proctor Valley Road. His large ranch grew its own feed, included lemon orchards, and devoted 500 acres to lima beans starting in 1917. In 1945, the Williams Ranch was sold to Union Oil Company of California.

Most of the 30 dairies in the valley were small operations, with 20–30 Holstein or Jersey milk cows. However, the Rollin Dairy that started on 160 acres of the Sam Williams ranch in 1945 grew into one of the largest producing dairies by the 1970s. The fan-shaped cattle pens and large central barn are pictured above. Paul Rollin and his family hosted annual 4-H Club events on the ranch.

Cloyed's Dairy opened the first "Dairy Drive-In" in San Diego on National Avenue in 1947, and it proved to be a popular idea, serving 1,000 cars a day with "Farm Fresh Milk" at 17¢ per quart. Two years later, the Harbor Drive-In opened on 25 acres of Cloyed Dairy land on the edge of the Sweetwater River between National City and Chula Vista.

The Few Acres Dairy was owned by Francis M. Brown, who started his dairy farm in 1915 on the southeast corner of Bonita Road and Otay Lakes Road, and by World War II, it had this fleet of trucks for home delivery. He sold his dairy in 1943 to Tom Eaton, who was the last dairyman to sell out to developers in 1975.

Ann (left) and Judy Gassaway ride their pony Comet to school in September 1948 from their home on Orchard Hill Road. Their brother Dana still lives on the hill. Their grandmother Josephine Loomis built her house down the hill on the edge of the Gassaway property. Josephine was postmistress of Bonita from 1949 to 1965.

Molly and Steve Gassaway sit with baby Ann and daughter Judy in 1943 when they started their house with a trailer and a small shack from the Boys School, where Steve had been headmaster until the school closed in 1942. They bought 12 acres on a hill with no roads for $100 per acre from Richard Allen, and over the next 20 years, they kept building on to and improving the house.

Kids ride their horses along one of the many paths that crisscrossed the valley in 1944. Leading is Bettsy Burch, followed in a row by Ruth Dunn, Kim Kirkpatrick, Margaret Ann Rogers, and Ann Stephens. The local newspaper reported in a story a few years later about "Bonita, Rural Haven" that "Bonita boasts more horses per capita than any community in southern California."

The hills around Sweetwater reservoir and the open country were much admired by the equestrians of the valley before housing developments filled in the space. Early morning rides by small groups such as this one around the reservoir were popular. The earthen dike on the south point of the reservoir can be seen in the lower right of this photograph. (Courtesy Bonita Valley Horsemen.)

Mary Barr starts a ride in 1975, leading on her horse Dandy, followed by Joanie Lester, through the gate in Rohr Park. The City of Chula Vista tried to prohibit horses from using some of the trails around the golf course, but protests from riders in the valley caused the city to modify its rules. (Courtesy Bonita Valley Horsemen.)

Joan Embery rode at a Bonita Valley Horsemen show in 1975. She was the goodwill ambassador from the San Diego Zoo who lived in Bonita in the 1970s and attended many of the equestrian events. (Courtesy Bonita Valley Horsemen.)

It was a common sight in Bonita to see groups of riders along Bonita Road stopping at the Bonita Village Shopping Center, which had hitching posts in front of stores. When the post office moved to Central Avenue in 1976, it provided hitching posts to serve horsemen and horsewomen mailing letters.

The Sunnyside Saddle Club was founded in 1963 by Noel and Shirley Confer and grew over the next 20 years into the largest riding club in the valley, with 500 members. This new ring opened in March 1984 at the east end of Rohr Park on land leased from the Optimist Club. (Courtesy Nancy Cornell.)

The Sweetwater Manor marker erected at Margaret Street and Sweetwater Road in 1929 represented the beginning of housing subdivisions that would replace farms and ranches with streets and yards and thousands of new homes. Developer Edward Anderson, a carpenter from Minnesota who had 12 siblings, named Margaret Street for his only daughter.

Nine

MODERN MANORS

Bonita began to change from rural to suburban with the first subdivisions by Ed Anderson and Albert Wheeler in 1929. Only a small number of homes were built in these "manors," as Anderson called them, until after the Great Depression and war years. The turning point came in 1949. Richard Allen started Bonita Acres, the first of 10 subdivisions opened by 1949. Alarmed residents formed the Sweetwater Valley Civic Association to set residential zoning at half-acre lots and to keep Highway 54 out of the valley. The SVCA did what it could to control growth, but modernization was relentless. The Ella B. Allen School opened in 1947. The South Bay Irrigation District, formed in 1951, would lead to public ownership under the Sweetwater Authority. The Bonita Sunnyside Fire District built its first station in 1951 on Bonita Road, joined by the Sweetwater Realty red barn in 1955. The Old Red Barn came down in 1960 for a new Bonita Village Shopping Center, and a massive apartment complex started to fill in the north side of Bonita Road. National City and Chula Vista began annexations that would slowly break apart the unincorporated valley community. Bonita's first sewer line was installed by 1963, permitting higher density growth. The "Million Dollar" golf course that was laid out in 1960 reshaped the center of the valley and attracted housing developments along the north and south rims. Corky McMillin's Bonita Highlands south of Central Avenue created new neighborhoods with streets, such as "Good Karma Lane," named after prize-winning horses. Otay Lakes Road connected the valley with Southwestern College, Bonita Vista High School, Rancho Del Rey, and the growing region of eastern Chula Vista. Tom Sefton opened the valley's first bank in 1964 where the railroad stopped to load lemons, and he found the old 174 rails under the street. By 1970, there were 48 commercial buildings in the valley where 20 years earlier there were only 7. The population in that short period had gone from 500 to 6,900. No longer was Bonita a refuge and haven from the modern world.

The McDade house in Sweetwater Manor at 5144 Sunnyside Drive was a small Spanish-style bungalow typical of the homes in Anderson's division, on lots of about 1.75 acres, intended to be affordable for the middle class. Coral McDade bought the house in 1941 and believes it was built by Charles Kelso, unlike other homes that were moved from another failed subdivision.

In this aerial photograph from 1961, some of the large Sweetwater Manor lots are starting to subdivide into smaller plots, especially along Nannette Street (named for Ed Anderson's wife) at the top center left, but the lots remain large along Sylvia Street (one of his six sisters) and Margaret Drive, top to right side. Margaret inherited the property and married Bernard Bernes of Chula Vista.

The Bonita Hills subdivision was created by Albert G. Wheeler from a 319-acre ranch to develop, according to the sign, "San Diego's Most Beautiful Suburb" for wealthy homeowners seeking "Social Restrictions" on large lots. Wheeler built his own home on the hilltop behind the sign and put a restriction in deeds that no other home could be higher than his.

The Wheeler residence, at its first address of 4005 Acacia Avenue, was built in 1928 on top of a 2.5-acre hill. The home was designed by Albert Treganza, who would design the Spanish Village in Balboa Park for the 1935 Exposition and the San Diego Police Station for the WPA in 1939. The colored Spanish tile in the entrance steps was used throughout the 15-room house.

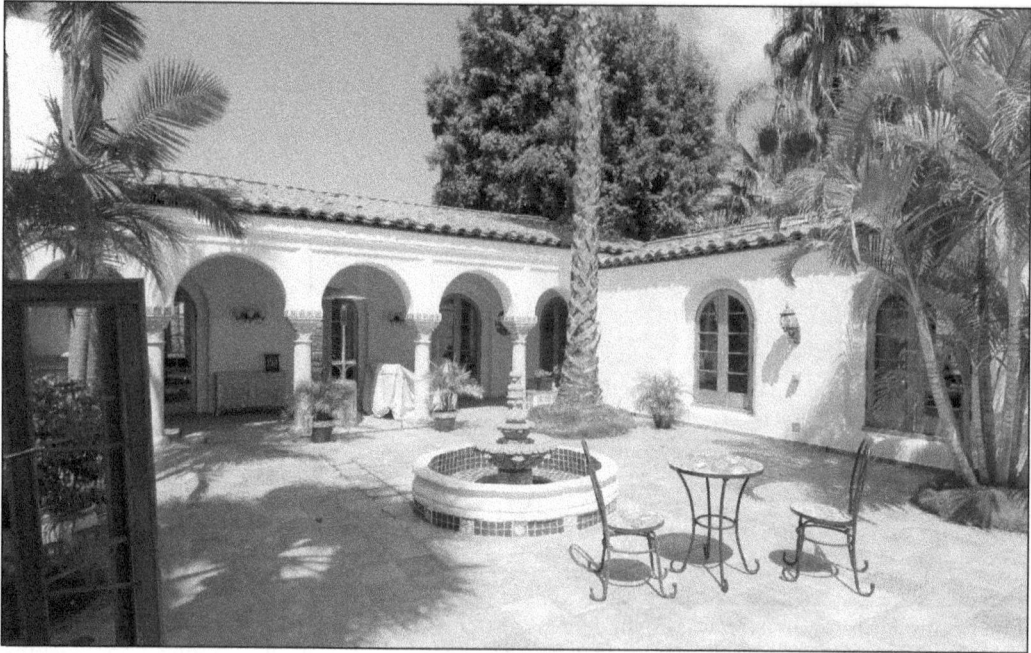

The Albert G. Wheeler house was built around a large central courtyard with two fountains and arched doors and windows. Wheeler hoped that as more rich families moved into his development, he would build a country club and a racetrack, but his dreams were ended by the Great Depression, and he died in 1934. Mrs. Shanny Wheeler lived in the house until 1977. (Courtesy Mario Modiano.)

The central courtyard's second fountain was inlaid with colored Spanish tile. To the right of this fountain was a tiled interior corner stairway that led, in 1928, from the ground-floor courtyard to a rooftop Moorish garden that has since been replaced with roof tile. (Courtesy Mario Modiano.)

The Spreckels house was built in 1932 by Albert Wheeler for resale purposes and was designed as a luxury house to attract wealthy buyers. It was sold in 1934 to John D. Spreckels III, the grandson of the John D. Spreckels who had owned the Coronado Hotel. The house was the most modern in Bonita, with electric heat, built-in vacuum cleaners, telephone, and intercom.

The great loggia spans the entire length of the Italian Mediterranean–style two-story stucco house on the north side, overlooking a pool that dates from the 1930s. After Spreckels, the house was owned by the president of Rohr, golfer Billy Casper, and after 1973 by Dr. Walter Shaw and his wife, Maria, who have restored and preserved its original beauty. (Courtesy Maria Shaw.)

The fire department in 1954 included, from left to right, (kneeling) Commissioner Charles N. Francis, Commissioner Robert O. Henschel, engineer William S. King, Robert Russell Jr., E. Scofield Bonnet, Mel Serniuk, and Commander ? Morris; (standing) Commissioner George C. Tim, Chief William Waters, Asst. Chief James W. Jones, Capt. Elmer C. Zinn, Arthur B. Cox, and Bert R. Hand Jr.

The fire station was built at 4035 Bonita Road in 1951. In this photograph from 1961, the trucks lined up are, from left to right, the most recent Engine No. 3, a Seagrave pumper; the old Engine No. 1, a 1954 Mack truck; and the smaller Engine No. 2, a Ford grass rig. On the right, four men stand next to the chief's station wagon parked by the Sweetwater Realty office, built in 1955 and patterned after the Old Red Barn.

114

Ingenious Jerry Gauss created Glarfs—dinosaur-like creatures made of steel, wire, concrete, and paint—and displayed them at his parents' house at Bonita and Valley Roads. This photograph is of the creature named Rumbi in 1959, when Jerry was a junior in Hilltop High School. Below he is working at his home on a Glarf in 1961. An orchard is planted across Sweetwater Road.

In 1963, while traveling from his job at Dinosaur Land in Alpine, Jerry was killed in an auto accident. When his parents moved from Bonita in 1969, they took the Glarfs with them, and they were lost for 30 years. In 1999, Patrolman Tom Everett found them in Chula Vista, and Phil Berdeski gave permission to move them to his Bonita Village Shopping Center.

Gordon Pettit (right) and Wesley Mohr look over new trees to be planted in 1960 on the 150-acre Bonita Valley Country Club (BVCC) golf course in the center of the Sweetwater Valley. This golf course became the catalyst for new housing developments on the north and south rims of the valley.

Billy Casper (right) shows the BVCC brochure to John W. Gardner, president of the new golf club in 1960. Billy went to Chula Vista High School and lived on Crela Street in Bonita with his wife, Shirley, and their three kids at that time. He and Gardner were among the 14 original members of the BVCC, along with Richard M. Allen, and Dick and Bob Wilson.

The BVCC clubhouse at 4548 Sweetwater Road was designed by architect William Lumpkins but only partially completed when opened in 1963. The City of Chula Vista annexed the golf course and Rohr Park in June 1966, and it became the Chula Vista Municipal Golf Course. In 1984, it was leased to American Golf Corporation.

The first Bonita golf course was built at the west end of the valley by Ray Koenig in 1956. This club moved in 1980 to the east end of the valley when National City annexed Koenig's land to build the Plaza Bonita Shopping Center. Part of the original clubhouse designed by Hank Bugenhagen was moved to become the sports bar connected to the new restaurant.

Ann Gassaway relaxes on construction pipe for the new South Bay Parkway in 1963, just north of her home on Orchard Hill Road. Her father, Steve Gassaway, opposed the highway and was one of the founders in 1949 of the Sweetwater Valley Civic Association, which persuaded the state to move the highway from the valley floor to this location beyond the north rim of the valley.

In 1986, Joe Schmidt drew this cartoon for the *Star-News* on the successful five-year fight by Capt. Richard Yokley and the Bonita Fire Department to reduce accidents on Highway 54 by having the state install a center divider. The highway had been expanded in 1984 with the construction of a flood control channel between I-5 and I-805.

The Erickson aerial of June 1934 shows the valley still rural and sparsely inhabited. The Willow Street Bridge at bottom center connected Bonita Road on the right and Sweetwater Road on the left. The old bridge route before the 1916 flood can be seen below the new bridge, forming a V with Bonita Road. The straight line of the old NC&O Railroad parallels Bonita Road. (Courtesy San Diego Historical Society.)

The aerial photograph of Richard Yokley about 1984 shows the La Bonita apartments along Bonita Road east of Willow. Housing developments cover the rims on both sides of the valley, and housing fills the Sunnyside–San Miguel area at the top.

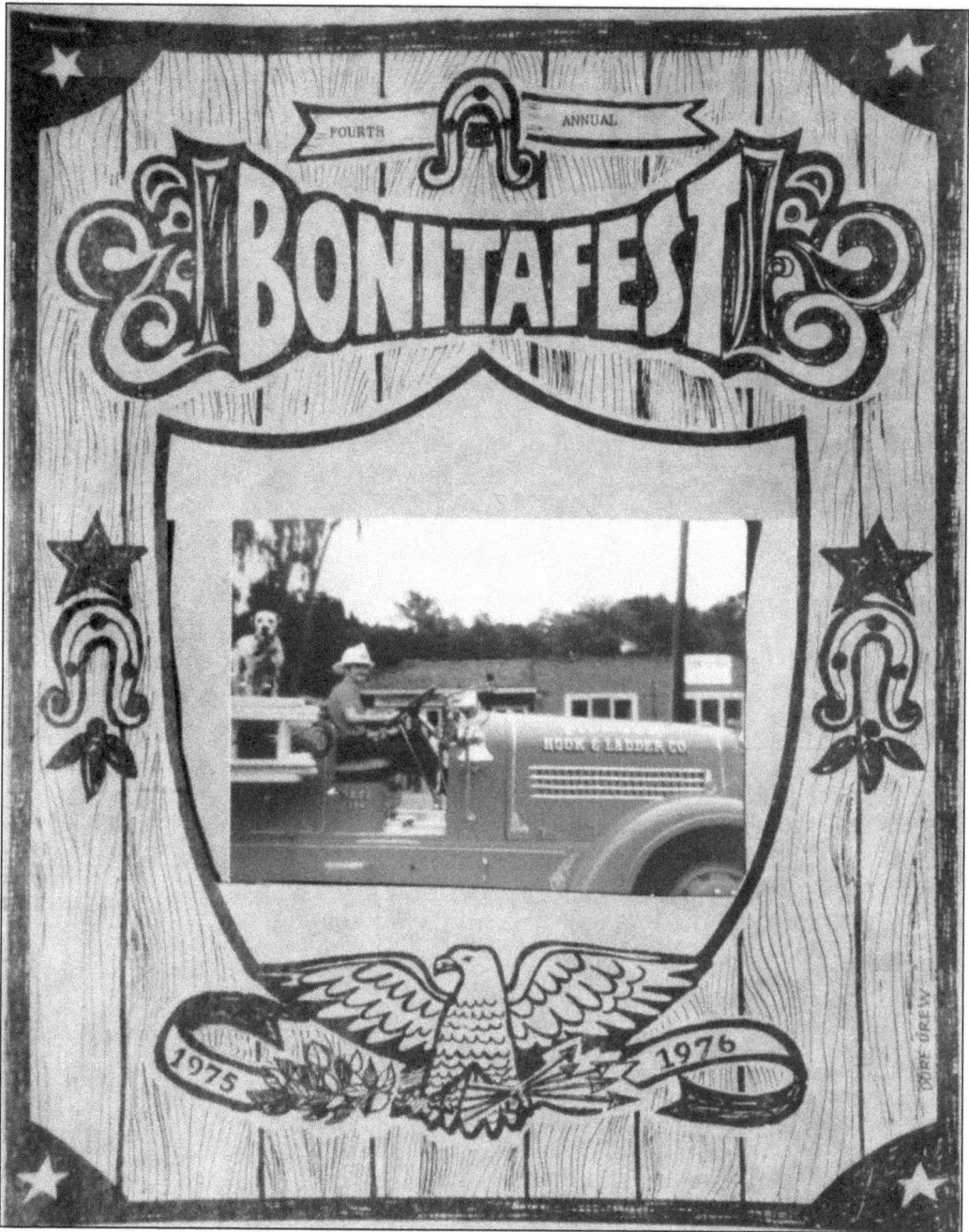

Dore Drew created this poster for the 1976 Bonitafest.

Ten

BONITAFEST

When she purchased Village Togs in 1971, little did Emily Ritter realize the whirlwind she had set in motion. It took Emily and her partner, Beth Marks, just weeks to realize that most of the Bonita merchants didn't know each other. Emily was soon canvassing the valley to get merchants to create the Bonita Business and Professional Association. Though the BBPA started strong out of the gate, attendance at meetings soon dropped. Emily suggested that they do something to get noticed, like have an Oktoberfest, and Adelle Rockwell suggested they call it "Bonitafest." Within minutes, the group was working on this new special event. The event commenced with music and square dancing in the street on Friday, October 19, 1973. Saturday, October 20, began with a flag raising at 8:00 a.m. and included Indian Guide Dancing and Drum Playing, a wine tasting, and an antique clothing fashion show. The old-time parade featured drill teams, bands, horses, and children pulling wagons carrying goats, chickens, and dogs. Many old-timers also rode antique cars in the parade, including grand marshals Commander and Mrs. Allan and Genevieve Olson, who had first come to the valley in the 1920s. In the years since 1973, Bonitafest has grown and evolved. In the late 1970s, Bonitafest lasted Friday evening through Sunday. In recent years, it has been shortened to one day. In 1978, Max Branscomb wrote the first melodrama, which was performed in a large tent erected on an empty lot, a tradition that continues to this day. In 1979, Pat and Kirk Dolan originated an Orange Crate Derby. For over 30 years, on the last Saturday in September, Bonita has put on its best face and celebrated its heritage. The Bonita Museum and Cultural Center started out as an historical photograph exhibit for Bonitafest. Through the generosity of the community, the City of Chula Vista, and the County of San Diego, the museum moved into a new building adjacent to the new Bonita Sunnyside Library in 2005. Preserving and celebrating the spirit of Bonita continues to be the museum's mission.

Though still part of the fire department's active fleet, the 1954 Mack Engine No. 1 was primarily used as a parade vehicle. This engine heads up Bonita Road at the first Bonitafest parade in 1973, with a small crowd on the sidewalk across the street from the new La Bonita Apartments.

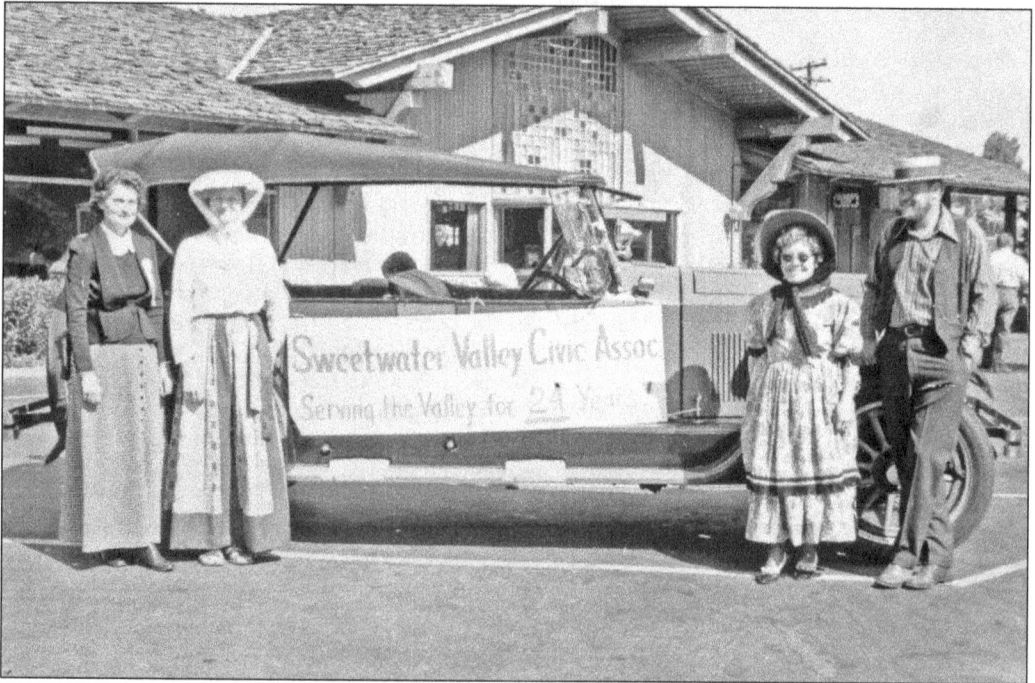

The Sweetwater Valley Civic Association had led the way in preserving the valley's rural nature and began the tradition of dressing in period costumes for Bonitafest in 1973. From left to right are Zula Pena, Carol Freno, Pat Spies, and Dick Hagen.

The judges and guests have preferred seating on the platform in front of Victor Wulff's new Bonita Valley Suites office building on Bonita Road for the 1973 Bonitafest parade.

Horsemen in Bonitafest 1973 march by the Sweetwater Realty building that was built in 1955 by Morris Allen, whose father was foreman at the construction of the original packinghouse barn. Allen built the copy in an attempt to preserve some of the historical lore of the Bonita area.

Bonitafest melodrama *Thin Skins and Hayseeds*, written and produced by Max Branscomb with Loren Lindsey Tarantino, brought Bonita history to life. In this 1978 photograph, David Harris played pioneer farmer Alf Lansley, and the Lansley family was played by Lisa Mercier (left) and Cora Powell (center), with an unidentified boy at right. (Courtesy Max Branscomb.)

Richard Pena and Zula Pena ride in the open wagon for the Bonita Museum in the Bonitafest parade. Richard helped Max Branscomb do the research for his melodrama by bringing together a group of old-timers who told their stories to Max. The melodrama is the longest-running theater production in San Diego history, performed every year since 1978.

Added in 1978, the Bonitafest Wine Tasting with dinner and entertainment was a popular addition. Nan Myers, holding the microphone, was the host for the 1980 dinner. Her husband, Ed Myers, is in the black hat, and Jan Taipale plays guitar.

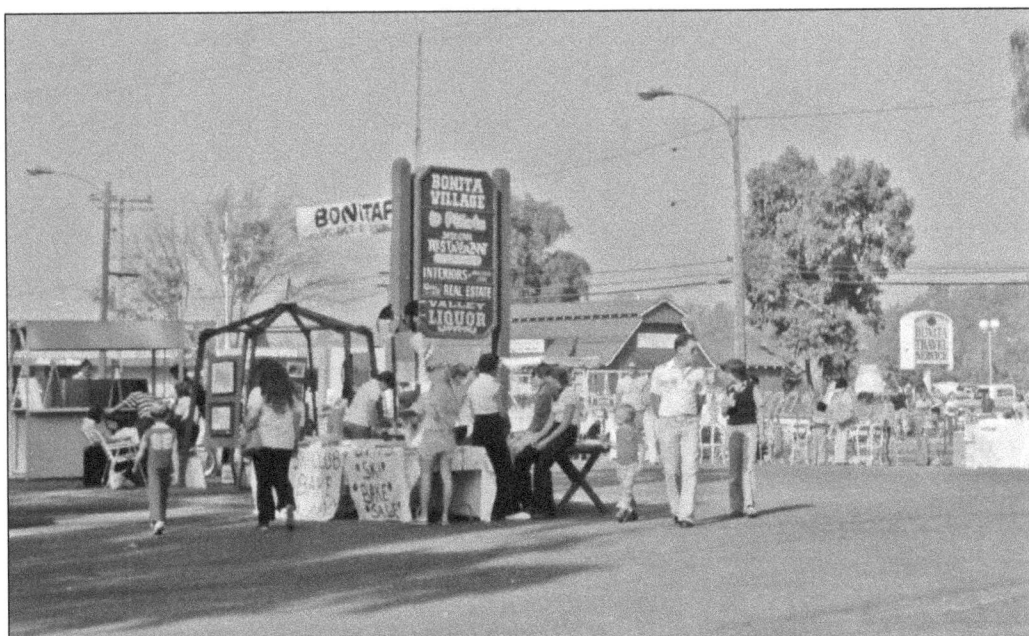

Local merchants and organizations set up booths along Bonita Road, selling arts, crafts, plants, and food to the visitors during the 1980 Bonitafest. Many local school and church groups raised money for special events as the Ski Club Bake Sale booth shows.

Started by Pat and Kirk Dolan in 1979, the Orange Crate Derby was a very popular addition to Bonitafest. Local boys and girls built their cars under strict rules of weight and steering and raced down the hills of Bonita. Derby entrants, with the winners at the front, participate in the 1993 Bonitafest parade.

The Bonita Museum opened in 2006 in a new building that was a joint project of the County of San Diego, City of Chula Vista, and the museum, with $250,000 in donations from the local community. The county matched funds by contributing $250,000.

This is the old Bonita village along Bonita Road near Willow Street in 1959, which would soon disappear. A shopping center will soon replace the Old Red Barn, a Jack in the Box will replace the Union 76 gas station, and apartments will go up along the road that will be widened to four lanes.

Visit us at
arcadiapublishing.com

www.ingramcontent.com/pod-product-compliance
Lightning Source LLC
Chambersburg PA
CBHW080601110426
42813CB00006B/1365